BATIK
AND OTHER PATTERN DYEING

LECTOR HOUSE PUBLIC DOMAIN WORKS

BATIK AND OTHER PATTERN DYEING

WALTER DAVIS BAKER,
IDA STRAWN BAKER

ISBN: 978-93-5420-151-6

Published: 1920

LECTOR HOUSE LLP
E-MAIL: lectorpublishing@gmail.com

BATIK
AND OTHER PATTERN DYEING

BY

WALTER DAVIS BAKER
AND
IDA STRAWN BAKER

OF
THE WALDCRAFT STUDIOS
INDIANAPOLIS, INDIANA

1920

THE PREFACE

ONE of the hopeful observations during the few years of applied art education in our schools has been the readiness with which educators have taken up and kept problems in which the mediums of expression were practical and efficient, suitable for the purpose intended, and the equal readiness with which they have dropped other problems.

The burning of wood as a means of decoration did not stand this test, therefore it had to go. Oil paint is not a suitable medium to decorate textiles, therefore it too has nearly fallen from use.

The value of applied art to home and community rests upon the test, whether the pupil who works out the problems becomes by virtue thereof a more useful and cultured individual in the home and in the social and industrial life of the community.

A problem which satisfies this test becomes a basic problem. To a pupil who has once bound a book with its cover design, end papers, etc., a book is a different thing ever after. He becomes a more intelligent and cultured member of the consuming public so far as books are concerned. To the demands of many such members the book binders respond with better things. Therefore book binding is a basic problem.

Similar reasoning applies when a student weaves a fabric, plans and makes an article of dress, a toy, a silver ring, or a poster.

No one will dispute that the all-over dyeing of a fabric, and the decoration of a textile with a dyed pattern, are basic problems. The recent war brought home the vital place that dyes hold in the life of the people.

As suitable materials have become available teachers have been eager to learn and use these problems.

It is seldom that an applied problem comes to the art teacher that offers in so full a measure the essential features of a basic problem as does batik work, which involves both all-over and pattern dyeing.

The mechanical process is rather simple and offers no especial difficulty, requiring only the painstaking care that good teachers exact from pupils.

The design element involved may be simple or elaborate, fitted to the capacity of the pupil. It is a real problem in design, however, allowing great freedom yet carrying with it the discipline of a later test, viz., applied expression within the limitations of definite mediums.

As the process controls the entire surface, the pupil is directed to plan his design and ground areas both in space and color relations. The mediums used are fabrics and dyes, both inseparably involved in education as they are in life. The pupil must plan for the use intended and also for the particular type of individual or scheme of decoration.

The work carries with it all along the anticipation of results; and the beautiful finished piece is the reward of effort. What more could be desired in an applied school problem?

The endeavor and the hope in presenting this little book on "Batik and Other Pattern Dyeing" is to help those who are learning to undertake these problems with breadth of thought and efficiency of method.

THE AUTHORS.

Indianapolis, Indiana.

CONTENTS

Chapter   *Page*

THE PREFACE. v

I. HISTORY AND CHARACTER OF BATIKS 1

II. PRINCIPLES OF DYEING FABRICS 21

III. WAX RESIST PROCESSES 31

IV. BATIKS AND OTHER ILLUMINATED TEXTILES 48

V. DYEING FOR PLAYS AND PAGEANTS 65

VI. TIE-DYED WORK. 75

VII. STICK PRINTING, BLOCK PRINTING AND STENCIL DYEING. . . .86

INDEX 98

THE ACKNOWLEDGMENTS

THE authors are pleased to express grateful indebtedness to a number of friends in Indianapolis.

To Miss Roda E. Selleck, Shortridge High School, for her advanced high school projects in the development and application of batik designs; also in the application of tie-dyeing and blown stenciling.

To Miss Carolyn S. Ashbrook, Shortridge High School, for her projects with an elementary high school class.

To Miss Olive Rush, who designed and executed "The Capture" for the frontispiece.

To Miss Blanche Stillson for assistance in illustrating the wax resist processes; also for her designs, the blouse, page 55, and the pattern, page 58.

To Mr. Charles E. Rush, Librarian of the Public Library, for securing valuable publications of the Dutch Government.

To Mr. George Somnes, Director of The Little Theater, and Mrs. Eugene Fife, Little Theater, for their work revealed in Chapter V.

For the loan of old textiles, Miss Eliza Niblack, Curator of Textiles, John Herron Art Institute, the sarong, page 49, and the chundri, page 76; Mrs. Clifton A. Wheeler, the Javanese patterns, page 64; Mrs. William O. Bates, the sarong design used for the end papers; Miss Florence Fitch, Director of Art, Public Schools, the Indian block printing, page 89.

For permission to photograph their own handicraft, Miss Mary Overbeck (Cambridge City, Ind.) the tie-dyed patterns, pages 78 and 79; Mrs. James Thompson, the costume jewelry, page 51, and the tie-dyed scarf, page 79; Mrs. J. R. Brant, the blouse, page 54; Miss Mary Janet O'Reilly, the camisole, page 51.

Now what I want to do is to put definitely before you a cause
for which to strive. That cause is the Democracy of Art, the ennobling of daily and common work, which will one day put hope
and pleasure in the place of fear and pain as the forces which
move men to labor and keep the world a-going.

·····William Morris

"THE CAPTURE," BY OLIVE RUSH

CHAPTER I
HISTORY AND CHARACTER OF BATIKS

T EXTILE art is one of the oldest arts known to man. Personal adornment was perhaps the first attempt at expressing beauty. Costume designing and textile industries are still most vital movements in the artistic development of the people.

Asia is the great mother of beauty in textile decoration. We do not talk or write about textiles without using the words of her ancient peoples.

"Batik"—this ancient Asiatic word—is one of the oldest crafts of the Orient. In India, Java and Japan the highest technique is reached. These people have made a great art of costuming. Each caste, religion and festival requires its special garment.

From the historic days when Columbus searched vainly for a shorter way to the fabled riches of the East Indies until the way was found, these treasure islands held the possessions most coveted by the Western World.

More than a thousand years before this time, the neighboring Hindus came to these rich islands bringing with them religious teachers, road makers and skilled craftsmen. Many expeditions fastened upon the native tribes the religion and culture of the older and more civilized country.

While the Spanish, Portuguese and English adventurers were discovering new lands and claiming them for their kings, the Dutch sailors carried to and fro the produce of the world. The Netherland warehouses were filled with treasures of the Orient.

Keeping pace with its industry were the universities and the common schools. The records and drawings of Dutch scholars disclose so much detailed information upon the handicraft industries of the day that the recent revival of batik is traced to their genius.

Books issued by the Dutch Government to promote the batik craft, picture Javanese women and girls seated upon fiber mats before a vertical frame upon which the material is hung for the execution of their art. Men too are at work printing and dyeing these fabrics. Housewives in staid processionals display the occupation. Princes and fine ladies disport their gorgeous costumes. Priests climbing the steps of their temples past the long rows of their sacred gods are resplendent in batik array. Their oldest gods are clothed in sculptured batik.

Designs of great beauty and skilled execution enrich the pages of these rare volumes.

Among the Dutch people much effort has been made to promote this art. Native designs have been fostered and the modifications have been in demand for European trade.

The American adaptation of batik has followed closely upon the European revival.

The Chinese, however, have control of the industry in Java. They employ natives at low wage to make batiks. The home occupation that took no account of time or pains is dying out. In a few years the products of this infinitely better craft will be found only in museums and in the possession of collectors. Under Chinese management batik making has become the leading occupation.

Batik is a method of drawing or painting with wax upon a fabric, after which the material is dyed and the wax removed. The result of this process is a decoration in silhouette upon the dyed background of the goods.

The wax generally used in Java is hot beeswax or a vegetable wax imported from Japan. The wax is removed by scraping and melting. The waxing is repeated as many times as there are colors in the design. The process is long and tedious and often requires months.

Formerly the colors were native vegetable dyes. The most common were indigo, mango tree bark and madder. These colors have fallen into disuse, artificial dyes having replaced them.

COSTUME OF AN UPPER CLASS JAVANESE WOMAN

The wax resists the action of the dye-bath except where it cracks. Here the dye creeps in, producing the characteristic "crackle" of batik work. The Oriental craftsman never forces crackle. With him it is always an incident, the subtle accident of his handicraft.

JAVANESE WOMAN ENGAGED IN BATIK DECORATION

The nature of the process forces simple execution in waxing the shapes and outlines, and also limits the number of times the piece may be dyed. Applying the wax becomes increasingly difficult after each dipping. Spotting of color over the entire piece makes thinking in color as important as the painting in of the wax.

The Oriental process of dyeing is the reverse of the American, in that it applies the darkest colors first. This necessitates previous waxing over parts to be kept light and also the removal of the wax and an entire new waxing after each dyeing. The American method is to dye the lightest colors first and build up the deeper colors. Between dyeings the old waxing is repaired and additional areas waxed.

The "sarong," worn by Javanese natives, is a skirt-like piece of goods about the size and proportion of a window curtain. This garment falls from the waist, or above it, to the feet. The fabric is cheap cotton manufactured in Holland or England. The color and decoration of the sarong is influenced by caste and religion. The feudal framework of Javanese society has given much significance to rank.

The women add to the sarong a "kemban." This garment is not unlike a blouse without shoulder supports or sleeves. The kemban is wound tightly about the body under the arms. The drapery covers the upper part of the sarong.

The "slendang" completes the wearing apparel of the women. It is a scarf worn for adornment or useful for carrying the youngest child, or other burdens.

The Javanese man wears the sarong in the same manner as the women, which leads the foreigner to awkward misunderstandings. His long hair is done on the top of his head and bound around with a "sarong kapala." This head dress is tied at the nape of the neck. The sarong kapala is square, and when fitted is starched and shaped to the head.

JAVANESE NATIVES DYEING BATIKS

Among the poorer classes these garments are plain, usually dark blue, for daily wear, but on occasions they are vivid with color decorations.

The native worker prepares his cotton goods by soaking in oil, afterwards in lye. This process is repeated until the material is softened and a pleasing yellow gray.

Hand decoration is done by women. The material is hung over an upright frame. The hand supports the goods, and the molten wax is applied to the design. They use a funnel-like cup with a bamboo handle. The wax trickles slowly through the slender tube, and with this the outline is made. This instrument is called a "tjanting." There is no right or wrong side of this fabric, as the waxing is done on both sides. To cover large surfaces with wax, they use a brush. These women have acquired a high degree of skill through repetition of the same design on the same kind of garment.

The wooden frame over which the goods are fastened is moveable. The wax is melted over an earthen heater with an open side, into which the ends of long sticks are thrust for burning.

JAVANESE MAN DECORATING A SARONG WITH A TJAP

Although the tjanting is the more desired and versatile device for applying wax, the men wax batiks with "tjaps." The tjap is a wooden block with designs of metal insert. The craftsman sits on a low stool in front of an inclined table over which the goods are smoothly spread. The bottom of a shallow pan is covered with wax, heated in the same manner as for the tjanting. An absorbent pad is placed in the pan, the tjap is pressed on the pad and imprinted on the fabric. The fabric is then turned and, with another tjap made like the first except with its symmetry reversed, wax imprints are made in exactly the same places. This insures good waxing on both sides of the fabric. The piece is then ready for the dye.

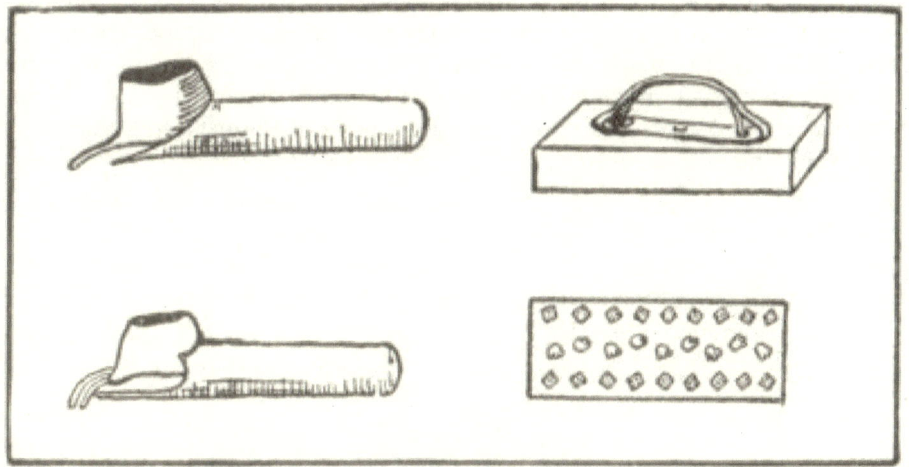

JAVANESE BATIK TOOLS

Sometimes a set of many tjaps is used to work out a pattern for a sarong or other garment. The making of these tjaps is the laborious and expensive work of experts. Of course we may expect to find many repetitions of such patterns, differing from one another only in the accidents of dyeing.

Frequently different methods of applying wax are used in the same decoration. Freehand work with the tjanting and brush on fine pieces serve to take away from the mechanical reproduction of tjap designs. The decoration of the end papers of this book, taken from a fine old sarong, affords an interesting study.

The most artistic and highly regarded effects in batiks among the Japanese workers are executed as they are in America today, *i.e.*, the wax is applied with a brush and is as free from mechanical aids as painting.

Pieter Mijer, in "Batiks and How to Make Them," published by Dodd Mead & Company, New York, writes of the modern development of batiks in Holland. The artists who have stimulated the present interest are Cris Lebeau, Dijesselhof and Lion Cachet. The illustrations of their work have a charm and individuality worthy of the highest respect. The author's own piece shown in the same group does not lose by comparison.

This book is also rich in valuable instruction and other illustrations of batiks, showing high American standards of the craft.

Batik adaptation in America is without tradition, and is an outgrowth of youth and enthusiasm caught up and carried on the high tide of progress and opportunity. The real significance of its popularity reaches backward into the necessity that confronted workers in textile designing after Europe was caught in the maelstrom of war.

The textile manufacturer has quickly adapted batik designs, indeed the artist working in batiks feels a close kinship to textile industry.

Batik decoration is free from limitations that restrict mechanical printing. In designing fabrics for the ordinary methods of mechanical reproduction, where great yardage is produced, the designer consults an average taste; whereas in batiks each piece is definitely designed with a particular setting or individual in view. There is no necessity for much repetition of any design, nor indeed can exact copy ever be made.

The first enthusiasm of the worker in batiks is apt to find expression in a burst of color run riot, of "crackle craze," with too little attention paid to design. But this soon gives way, as it should, to more conservative expression in which design is the controlling element, and the art comes to its own as a method of subtle and beautiful illumination of textiles.

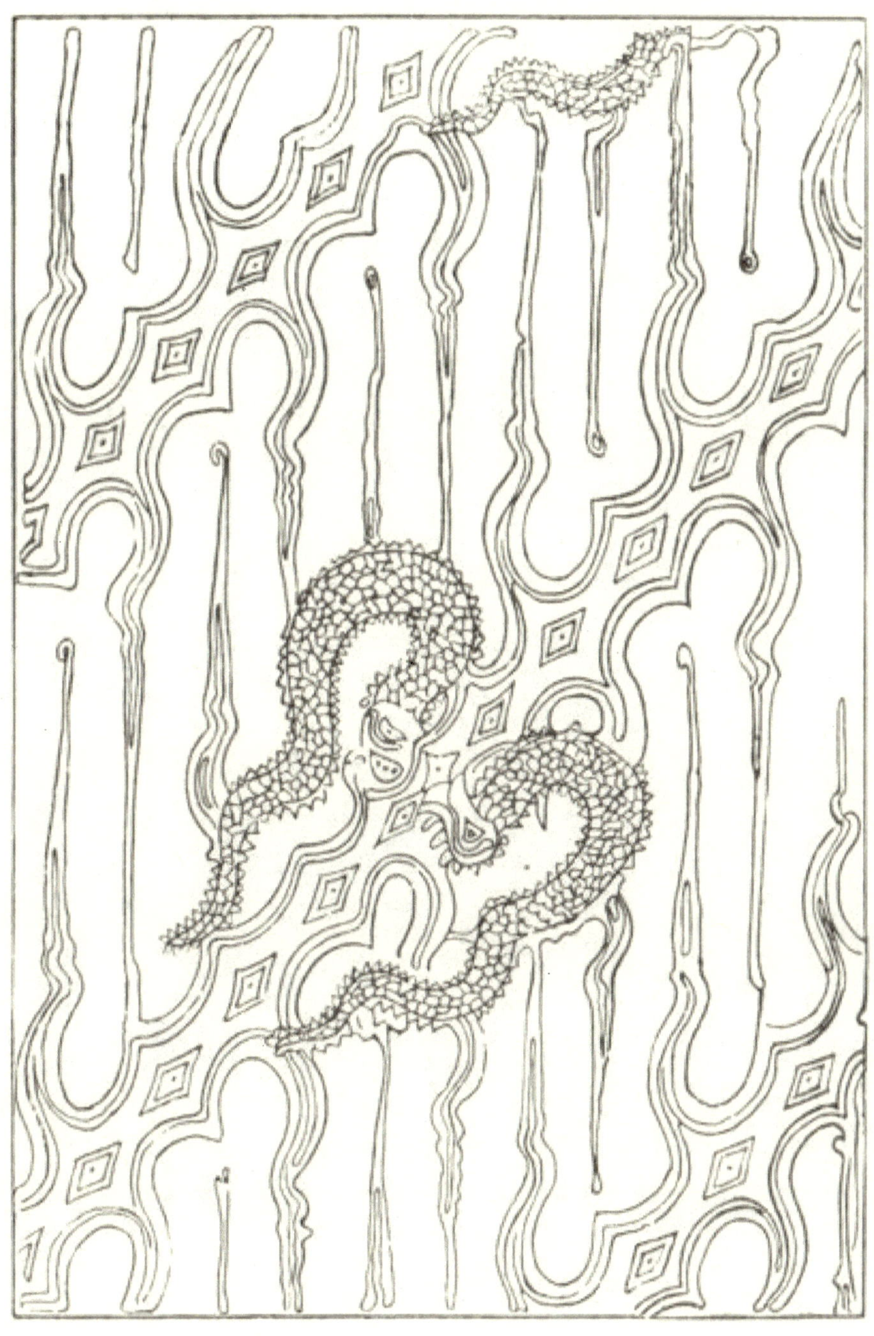

OLD BATIK DESIGN

OLD BATIK DESIGN

OLD BATIK DESIGN

OLD BATIK DESIGN

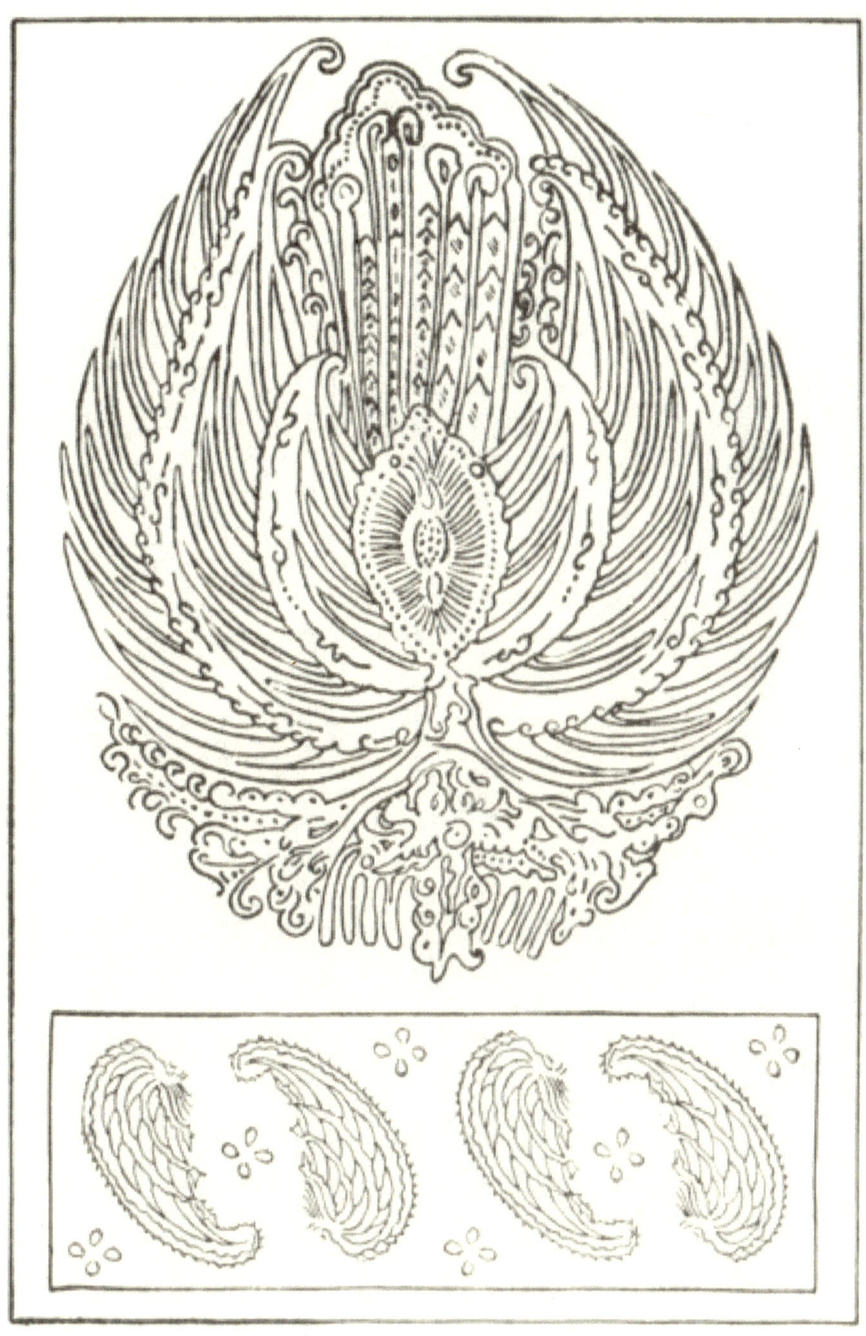

OLD BATIK DESIGNS

OLD BATIK DESIGNS

OLD BATIK DESIGNS

OLD BATIK DESIGNS

OLD BATIK DESIGNS

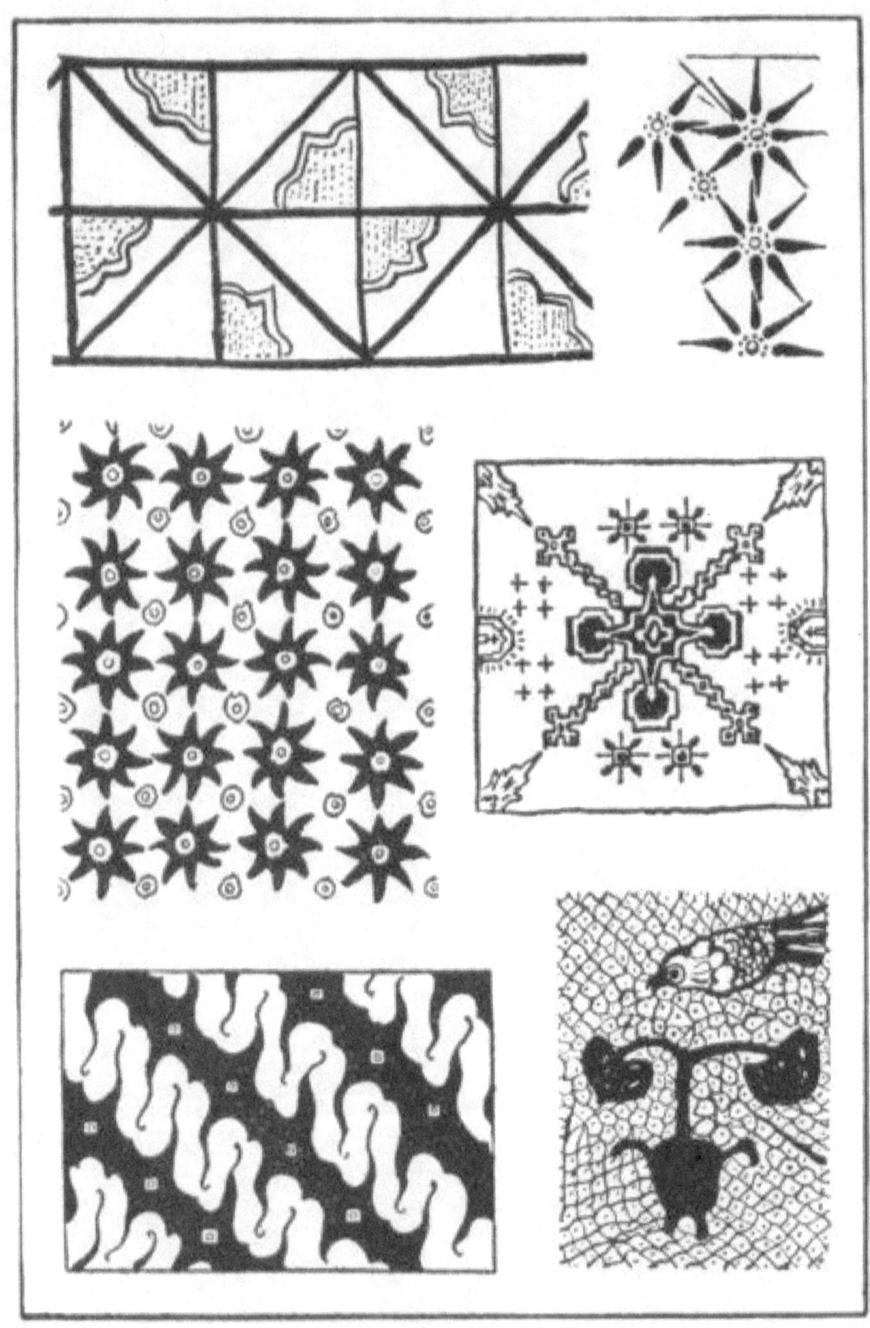

OLD BATIK DESIGNS

OLD BATIK DESIGNS

OLD BATIK DESIGNS

CHAPTER II
PRINCIPLES OF DYEING FABRICS

ALL-OVER DYEING

T HE simplest process of dyeing a fabric consists in submerging it in a solution of dye, known as a "dye-bath," and allowing it to extract or exhaust the color from the bath. It is necessary that there be an attraction or affinity between the fiber of the fabric and the dye in solution. All parts of the fabric must be given equal opportunity to extract the dye in order that a uniform color or "level" dyeing be obtained.

To accomplish this end experience has found that a few simple things must be observed. These have to do with, (1) the preparation of the fabric for dyeing, (2) the making of the dye-bath, (3) the handling of the fabric while in the dye-bath, and (4) the handling of the fabric after the dyeing.

1. *The Preparation of the Fabric.* The fabric must be clean. A spot of grease or other soil allows that part of the fabric less opportunity to extract color from the dye-bath, with the result that the dyeing is not level. Thorough washing with soap and warm water followed by a good rinsing will remove most spots. The methods

of the dry cleaner will be necessary for others.

All sizing must be removed. Sizing consists of substances such as clay, flour, starch, gum, oil, tallow, soap, etc., put into the fiber, either before or after weaving, for the purpose of giving weight, body, strength, stiffness, softness, finish, or other desired quality. Some sizing prevents the extraction of color from the dye-bath. In other cases the sizing itself absorbs a large share of the color, and later when the sizing is removed by washing this color goes with it. Vigorous washing with soap and hot water, followed by rinsing, will remove most sizing. A fabric which suffers injury by the removal of its sizing is not suitable for dyeing.

Previously dyed fabrics are often uneven in color due to spotting and fading. Level dyeing cannot be done over such color. The practice of the professional dyer is to remove or level this color before attempting further dyeing. This often calls for skill beyond that of the inexperienced worker. Sometimes prolonged boiling in strong soap suds will accomplish this. Many colors will also yield to hot hydrosulphite solution followed by a good rinsing.

Of course where goods have been previously colored there are limitations as to the colors that may be obtained by additional dyeing. For example, blue goods cannot, without the removal of the blue color, be dyed yellow but may be dyed green or purple or a deeper blue. Yellow goods cannot be dyed pink, but may be dyed orange, green, brown or black. This will be discussed more fully later.

Some fibers are hard and harsh and resistant, like crash and most new cotton cloth. This is due to the presence of gums, resins, waxes and other impurities, substances which either attract dyes or else prevent their taking the fiber. It is not possible to dye such goods successfully without first rendering the fibers soft and absorbent. This may be accomplished by prolonged boiling in washing soda. Repeated washing and exposure to air will also do it, hence old cotton usually dyes well. Technically there are elaborate and carefully carried out chemical processes of preparing cotton cloth for dyeing, and entire mills are busy doing this one thing.

The Javanese and other Oriental peoples purchase cotton cloth from Europe and treat it for many days, alternately soaking in oil and boiling in lye from ashes, then exposing to the hot sun. This process is repeated until the cloth is soft and absorbent and suitable to receive color decoration.

The cloth should always be thoroughly wet before putting it into the dye-bath. This should be done in water of the same temperature as the dye-bath.

It may be briefly mentioned here that a fabric must sometimes be given a treatment with some chemical, called a mordant, before it will exhaust certain dyes from the bath and be properly dyed.

2. *The Making of the Dye-Bath.* For simple dyeing, as mentioned at the beginning of this chapter, we must observe the following things:

The dye-bath must be sufficient in quantity to cover the goods well and to permit of their being worked thoroughly during the process of dyeing.

For the "dye-vat," or container for the dye-bath, use preferably a large graniteware pan or stone jar. Metal dishes, especially iron, are sometimes injurious.

Professional dyers often use vats of copper, brass or wood.

Soft water is preferable, and it should be free of sediment. The presence of iron in water is most injurious as it dulls, or "saddens," the shade of most colors. A hard water containing lime should be purified or softened. Lime sometimes causes uneven dyeing.

The dye must be completely dissolved in the water. If specks of undissolved dye are present there will be a spotted uneven dyeing. It is best to dissolve the dye in a small amount of water in a separate dish and then strain it. This should be added to the dye-bath a portion at a time during the dyeing. The reason for this will appear later.

The temperature of the dye-bath has much to do with the dyeing. There is no general rule applicable to all dyes. Each dye is usually accompanied by directions as to the temperature to be used. In general it may be said that all dyes work better in warm or hot solution. Some dyes require prolonged boiling; in other cases boiling is positively injurious to the dye. Sometimes a definite temperature below the boiling point must be maintained. Sometimes the temperature is raised or lowered during the dyeing. In all cases the temperature should be kept the same in the different parts of the bath, otherwise the dyeing will be uneven.

Many dyes, while most successful at high temperature, work very well in moderately warm, or even cold solution. This is of very great advantage in pattern dyeing, as in batik work, where the wax forbids a high temperature.

The composition of the dye-bath is not often as simple as we have indicated. Usually the dyer adds one or more other chemicals to assist in dissolving the dye, to control the rate of absorption of the dye by the fabric, or for some other purpose.

Some of the finest dyeing is done in baths so complex and with operations so exacting in care that only the trained professional with his elaborate equipment is able to undertake it.

3. *The Handling of the Fabric in the Dye-Bath.* Since all parts of the fabric must have equal opportunity to be dyed, in order that a level dyeing be obtained, it is absolutely necessary that the goods be worked as long as they remain in the dye-bath. This working must be thorough and continuous without interruption. This cannot be emphasized too much.

Let us think what happens if this rule is not heeded and the goods stand a few minutes in the bath. Some parts of the fabric will lie inside the folds of other parts and, having access to only a small part of the dye-bath, will soon exhaust all of the dye available, a condition known as "local exhaustion." Meanwhile other parts of the fabric more favorably situated will continue to absorb dye. More uneven dyeing in schools and homes is due perhaps to this cause than to any other.

Constant working of the goods keeps the dye that yet remains in solution uniformly distributed in the bath so that all parts of the fabric are absorbing dye alike. It also maintains what is equally essential to level dyeing, a uniform temperature in all parts of the bath.

It is to minimize the danger of uneven dyeing due to this local exhaustion that the dye-bath must be made of sufficient volume to cover the goods well. The goods must be moved about in the bath with the greatest freedom.

It is for the same reason, especially when the affinity between fiber and color is very great, that the dye is added a small portion at a time. The goods after being treated with part of the dye are lifted out of the bath, a new portion of dye quickly added and stirred, and the dyeing operation renewed. This is repeated until the desired shade is obtained.

The beginner is apt to think that to get a full color requires a concentrated dye-bath. Experience will teach him that, when the dyes are properly chosen for his fabric, a full color is obtained better by a longer treatment in a dilute bath, with additions of dye as mentioned above. In this way nearly if not all of the color put into the bath is absorbed by the cloth. This serves for economy of color, makes observation and control of the process easier, simplifies the problem of rinsing, and improves the quality of the dyeing. It is the only way dyeing to shade can be accomplished.

A slow dyeing is generally more level and successful in every way. In cases where the fiber absorbs the color greedily the dyer sometimes puts other ingredients called "assistants" into the bath to retard this absorption.

Frequently the craftsman does shaded dyeing, such as a scarf with deep blue ends grading to a light blue center. The following directions will accomplish this: Hold the scarf in the middle with one hand, dip the ends into the dye-bath and work them thoroughly with the other hand. Then lower the scarf into the bath very gradually without interrupting the working. If a half hour is taken to lower the scarf the ends will be in the bath perhaps thirty-five minutes, the center five minutes, and besides, before the center is dyed most of the color will have been exhausted from the bath.

4. *The Handling of the Fabric After the Dyeing.* The usual procedure after dyeing is a thorough rinsing to remove all surplus dye and chemicals. The importance of this will be appreciated from the following considerations:

If not removed many chemicals which have been used as assistants, becoming more concentrated as the goods dry, act injuriously on the dye or the fiber. Likewise any unused color will continue to dye the goods and of course unevenly. It is clearly essential that the rinsing be done immediately upon removal of the goods from the bath. The directions sometimes call for washing in soap and water after dyeing.

The excess of rinse water should be removed and the goods dried as rapidly as possible. Usually there is no objection to wringing. A fabric should never be allowed to hang and drain dry, as the dyeing is liable to become uneven in streaks, especially when the dye used is one given to run or "bleed," or in any case where the rinsing has not been absolutely thorough. The craftsman in dyeing a small piece frequently puts it between towels or newspapers to absorb the excess water and then shakes it until dry. This is to be commended. The technical dyer has suitable machinery to accomplish this work.

To dry a batik piece, where the wax forbids wringing or rough handling in any way, spread the piece carefully on towels or newspapers, cover with more towels or papers to remove the excess water, then shake very gently until dry, or hang on a waxed line.

At no time during the process of dyeing should the goods be allowed to remain in contact with other absorbent surfaces, such as boards, paper, cloth, clothes-line, grass, etc. These are apt to absorb color away from the goods and leave faded streaks or spots. A clothes-line used for this purpose should be waxed to make it non-absorbent.

PATTERN DYEING

The preceding general principles have been outlined with all-over dyeing especially in mind. We now come to the consideration of pattern dyeing, where in order to produce a design it is necessary to dye chosen parts of the fabric and keep the dye away from other parts. All that has been said with reference to making all-over dyeing efficient applies equally well to pattern dyeing. If possible, everything that is done to make all-over dyeing successful should be done in pattern dyeing to obtain a corresponding success.

Practically, however, we find it impossible to carry out some of the steps. For example, in the usual block printing, we do not have the problem of handling the fabric in a dye-bath, but rather that of handling dye on the fabric. Here we must take special steps to get the dye well into the fiber and secure the results obtained from the large dye-bath in all-over dyeing.

The fabric must be prepared for pattern dyeing in the same manner as for all-over dyeing. It is just as essential that it be clean, free of sizing, with its fibers soft and absorbent. Attention has been called to the pains taken by the Orientals in the preparation of their fabrics for decoration. We must not jeopardize our success by omitting to boil out new raw material and to clean old material.

This washing before dyeing also brings about any shrinkage that is to occur, and of course this must be done before the design is traced on the cloth, otherwise one could not intelligently work to dimensions.

A dyed pattern may be produced in several ways:

1. The dye is applied to the desired parts of the fabric and means taken to set it there without it spreading to other parts. This is known as direct coloring. Block printing and stenciling, as ordinarily done, are examples. Calico printing is an industrial application of the method.

2. A resist of some kind is applied to parts of the fabric to prevent their taking the dye, after which the fabric is treated in a dye-bath. Batik decoration and tie-dyed work both fall in this class. Stencils and print blocks may also be used in the application of the resist.

3. A "discharge" is put on parts of previously dyed goods, which either removes the color where it touches, or else alters the shade. Different discharges are used according to the nature of the dye and the goods. Some chemicals used

as discharges are liable, unless skillfully handled, to attack and tender the cloth. The method belongs rather to the industrial world where abundant apparatus and trained dyeing chemists are available. It is not, however, beyond the skill of a good craftsman who has acquired some experience with dyes.

The dye for direct coloring is applied in liquid form, sometimes thickened into a paste by use of gums, starch, etc. Often mordants or other assisting chemicals are incorporated into the mixture. In block printing this color mixture is brushed on the block, which is then imprinted on the fabric in the desired place, and the color driven into the fiber with pressure or a sharp blow. Stenciling is done by brushing the color mixture through the open parts of the stencil, or by blown stenciling in which a volatile color mixture is sprayed with an atomizer.

The best method of setting the dyes in this direct coloring is that pursued commercially in calico printing, treatment with dry steam, *i.e.*, steam applied at a temperature sufficiently high to prevent its condensation into drops of hot water on the fabric, which would be quite ruinous to the design. This is done successfully by Oriental craftsmen, and it would be very desirable to have suitable apparatus in American schools and studios.

Next best, though considerably less efficient, is the commonly practiced method of laying the fabric between dampened cloths and pressing with a hot iron until dry.

The resist method has an advantage in that it allows the use of a dye-bath. The limitation of temperatures that may be used places some restriction on the choice of dyes. Batik dyeing must be done without melting the wax resist. But after eliminating those dyes which require high temperatures and also those not suitable for pattern dyeing, there still remains a good range of colors. Batik is without doubt the most versatile of all methods of pattern dyeing.

Tie-dyed work depends upon tightly wound string or yarn to resist the dye. It also has the advantage of the dye-bath. Though less versatile than batik, it has a time-honored place as a method of beautiful and charming results. The introduction of sticks over which the tying is done, such sticks as are used by the children in stick printing, has opened new problems with added variety and much interest.

DYES

The colors available for craft work are commonly grouped into the following classes, which will be briefly described:

Direct Colors. These are so called because they are applied to all fibers directly without the use of mordants. They are principally used for dyeing cotton. Some dyes of this class have affinity for both cotton and wool. Most of the package dyes sold at the local stores are of this class. They are applied to cotton in a boiling bath and to wool at high temperature near the boiling point. Different assistants are used varying with the dye and the nature of the fabric.

The direct colors, being very soluble, are prone to "bleed" when the goods are washed, but owing to this same fact it is easy to produce level dyeing on the goods.

On this same account, however, and also on account of the high temperature required, they are not well suited for pattern dyeing.

Acid Colors. These have great commercial value for dyeing wool and sometimes silk. The best of them are quite fast to light but not to washing. They are not suitable for cotton or linen.

Basic Colors. These will dye wool and silk directly and also raffia, straw, basketry material, leather and wood. They dye cotton when mordanted with tannic acid, and this constitutes a very large commercial use. Basic dyes are especially strong in coloring power. Many of them are fugitive to light. A few of the best of them, however, when properly applied, are fast to washing and fairly fast to light.

Sulphur Colors. These are used extensively on cotton, giving colors fast to washing and to light. The dyeing is done at high temperature in a strongly alkaline bath of sodium sulphide along with other assistants. The colors are all dull and the range of colors is not complete, there being a lack of reds. These dyes are not suitable for silks.

Vat Colors are so called because the method of dyeing is that of the indigo vat. Indigo has been known for a long time, but only in recent years have other dyes of this class been produced, until now the series includes the entire range of colors. As a class they are the fastest colors ever known. The best of them are so fast that the cloth will wear out without the color changing. They are used chiefly on cotton and linen, sometimes on silk.

Vat dyes have been very expensive and scarcely obtainable during the war. Their future is of great interest and importance both in the industries and to craft workers.

In addition to the dyes above mentioned there are many others the use of which is quite complicated and technical and therefore confined to the industries.

For a fuller discussion of dyes and their uses the reader is referred to Pellew's "Dyes and Dyeing" (Robert McBride & Co., New York). This is a most excellent book written for craftsmen. Like most of our literature, the treatment of dyes is based upon pre-war conditions, when nearly all of our colors were imported. The latest edition, however, contains an added chapter dealing with the present transitional state, incident to the transfer of the industry to this side of the water and the development of great American color houses.

It may be added that the leading firms carrying school art supplies offer dyes in suitable form especially adapted for the problems in pattern dyeing.

Perhaps a few suggestions to the less experienced of our readers will prove helpful. All of the good dyes manufactured today are in a very pure form. The use of one dye alone often gives results that are crude without any subtle beauty. It is frequently necessary to apply the principle well known to all workers in color, that colors are softened and beautified by small admixtures of their compliments; that one color that is cold, or another that is hot, becomes warmed or toned by a suitable admixture of other colors.

It may be stated that most of the beautiful dyeing is built up from two or more colors. This is accomplished, according to the nature of the dyes and the fabric, by mixing the colors in the same dye-bath, or by dyeing the cloth successively in different colors. Of course the previous condition of the fabric must be taken into account. A bleached cotton cloth must be treated differently from a grayed one if an equally soft effect is desired.

In the old days dyes contained impurities which often caused beautiful grayed effects. But it is inexcusable today for anyone with knowledge of the above principle and with elementary knowledge of dyes and dye-baths not to get equally good results.

The inartistic work that we see so prevalent today in the realm of dyed fabrics is due in part to ignorance and lack of appreciation of good color and in part to the commercial race for profit. As the taste of the people makes demand for better things the response of industry will not be wanting.

Nor need the craftsman of today spend idle time mourning the disappearance of vegetable colors and his necessity for using coal tar dyes. We must remember that only the best of the vegetable dyeing has come down to us. The proportion of poor work with vegetable dyes has always been as large or even larger than with the present-day colors. We are too prone to compare the ordinary home dyeing of today or the cheaper commercial dyeing with the good pieces that have been preserved from the past. When in justice the comparison is made of the best with the best, the coal tar dyes not only do not suffer but they really gain.

The coal tar dyes are like the vegetable dyes in the sense of being organic. In many instances they are identical chemically with corresponding dyes formerly obtained from vegetables. The one difference, as we have indicated, is their purity. Just as our granules of sugar have displaced the sweetening of former days; just as our modern medicines have succeeded the herb-teas of our grandparents, so also have come our dyes. All are achievements of science.

Coal tar dyes have come to stay, vegetable dyes for the most part have gone and will not return, and there is no sadness in the word. It is rather for us to rise to the challenge that has come, to recognize our greater heritage, and by pains, patience and intelligence in our work to ply the art worthily.

COLOR MIXING

The following general principles of color mixing apply to dyeing, both when colors are mixed in a dye-bath and when they are dyed one color over another:

Red is grayed by small amounts of yellow and blue or by any color containing both of these, as green, brown or gray.

Yellow is grayed by small amounts of red and blue or by any color containing both of these, as purple, brown or gray.

Blue is grayed by small amounts of red and yellow, or by any color containing both of these, as orange, brown or gray.

Red plus yellow gives orange or yellowish red or reddish yellow. These are grayed by a small amount of blue or any color containing blue, as green, purple, brown or gray.

Red plus blue gives purple or reddish blue or bluish red. These are grayed by a small amount of yellow or any color containing yellow, as orange, green, brown or gray.

Blue plus yellow gives green or bluish yellow (usually called greenish yellow) or yellowish blue (usually called greenish blue). These are grayed by a small amount of red or any color containing red, as orange, purple, brown or gray.

Red plus yellow plus blue give—

(1) One of the above if any one or two of the three is present in the small proportion necessary for graying purposes.

(2) Gray if all three are present in such proportion as to neutralize each other. If this is perfectly accomplished we have a neutral gray, otherwise a red gray, yellow gray, blue gray, purple gray, etc. Gray intensified becomes black, and there are modified blacks, as blue black, green black, etc. In making up a gray or black, beginners usually err in taking too large a proportion of yellow, and perhaps also of red.

(3) Brown if the three are present within certain other ranges of proportion. Browns may be classified as yellow browns, red browns, blue browns, green browns, purple browns, etc.

There are all gradations between neutral gray and the browns; between the browns and the secondary colors, orange, green and purple; between the secondary colors and the primary colors, red, yellow and blue.

In the practical handling of dyes, in order to get the entire range of colors from the primary colors, it is necessary that the red, yellow and blue dyes chosen be pure and luminous in color quality. Fortunately, there are such dyes.

There are, however, other valuable dyes that do not have this purity of color. For example, there are yellows containing considerable red or brown, reds containing yellow or blue, blues containing red, etc. Then there are dyes that are green, brown, purple and black. All of these have limitations when used in compounding colors. Neither a yellow inclined to the brown, nor a red containing blue, can be used to form a luminous orange. Likewise the compounding of a vivid blue green, or reseda green, forbids either the yellow or the blue containing any appreciable admixture of red.

All of these dyes find great use in the industries, and all of them, within their limitations, are valuable for color mixing. Having acquired a working knowledge of red, yellow and blue dyes, it will be found of practical benefit to include some of the others. An experienced craftsman works with a small range of colors chosen for his particular purpose.

Dyes differ in coloring power, even different specimens of the same dye, so that it is not possible to give quantitative formulas for certain colors bearing popular names. It will be helpful to discuss a few of them.

Olive green may be made by adding to blue-green either red or preferably yellow brown. This addition should be made a little at a time with frequent tests, a suggestion applicable to all color mixing.

Tan is obtained by mixing yellow and yellow brown. An added tinge of blue or green gives pongee.

Gold contains much yellow with certain smaller amounts of red and blue. But it might be difficult to control the addition of these colors, so it is better to start with much yellow and add a little at a time orange and blue green.

For burnt orange add yellow brown to orange.

For turquoise add to blue a little yellow, or preferably blue green.

For old rose add to dilute red a tinge of blue or preferably purple.

Taupe is a gray thrown off, usually with purple, but sometimes with red or yellow or blue.

Salmon is formed by adding to yellow some orange and a tinge of brown.

Any dyeing over old color must be considered as a mixing of the new color with the old, which manner of thinking will help in choosing the dye necessary for a desired effect. For example, a green cloth is to be dyed black. There should be two dyeings, the first a red to neutralize the green, the second a black to intensify the neutrality. Likewise a red cloth becomes black by dyeing first green and then black.

Over a light yellow purple may be dyed, the result will be a grayed purple. Over a strong yellow much purple will be required and the result will be a very much grayed purple approaching if not becoming a purple black.

In batik decoration by successive dyeings the craftsman is constantly mixing the new dye with that already in the fiber. Having once introduced an intensity of any primary color, yellow, red or blue, he must thereafter, unless he removes this color, complete his pattern by producing secondary and tertiary colors.

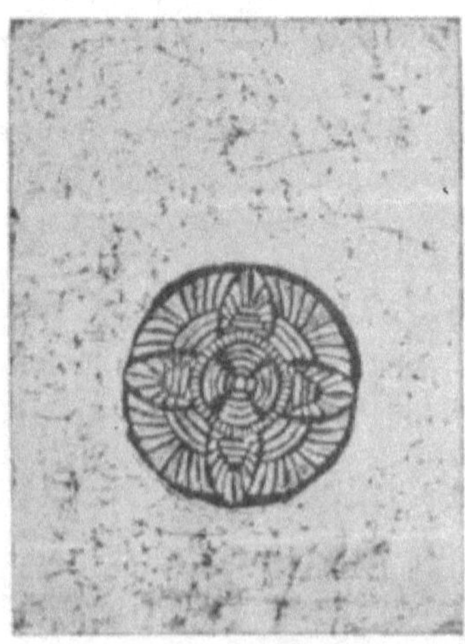

CHAPTER III
WAX RESIST PROCESSES

THE most commonly used fabrics for batiks are thin silks, white or light in color. Wax penetrates the sheer materials better. They take the color more evenly, and retain their brilliant texture. Heavy materials must be waxed on both sides to insure perfect stopping out of color.

The design is more easily applied to thin goods, as the decoration is readily traced. On heavy fabrics the design is either drawn free hand or pounced. When the outline is drawn in wax the drawing does not disappear in the dyeing. When only parts of the design are painted in with wax the outline must be redrawn after each dyeing. For this purpose pouncing is best.

Velvets should be stopped out on the wrong side. Steaming will raise the pile again, or it may be sent to the dry cleaner.

A BATIK FRAME

AN OUTLINE DRAWING IN WAX

Wood is a good medium to take wax resist. The wax is removed by scraping. The surface is cleaned with gasoline and finished in any approved manner. Toys, frames, trays, basket bottoms, boxes, etc., are very pleasing when decorated in this manner.

COLOR PAINTED WITHIN WAX OUTLINES

Leather and paper are dampened and pasted smoothly on glass. They are then decorated like wood.

Chiffons and crepes may be waxed double, or even folded four times.

In applying a design, care should be taken to keep the fabric straight. Drawing a thread from the fabric makes a good guide.

When working upon woven materials it is best to use a frame placed horizontally upon a table. A frame suitable for this work should be light to handle and strong. It should be high enough above the table to keep the wax or dye from touching it. When the wax touches an obstacle before it is cold it sticks. The wax is apt to break when pulled away from the object. Color penetrates by accident and the result is disappointing. Some artists work on a table upon which smooth or glazed paper is spread. Here again the wax may also suffer. When dyes are painted on the fabric, if they touch the table or other objects they spread and mar the definite outline of the design.

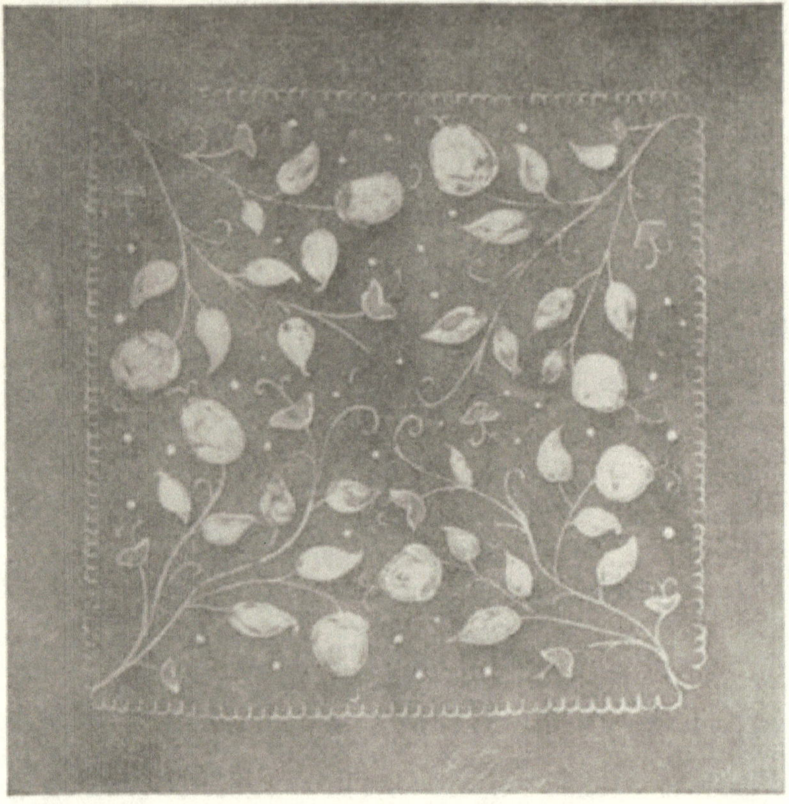

THE COMPLETED PATTERN

A frame, around the inside edge of which are cloth strips for pinning or sewing the fabric securely, is an excellent aid to good workmanship. Adjustable holes with corners secured by screws and wing nuts make it possible to roll long pieces of cloth at the top and bottom of the frame. Or by means of these holes the strips may be spliced together to form a still larger frame.

Paper should be rolled with the cloth to prevent the wax sticking. Handled in this manner only a small part of the work needs to be exposed, and the work can be done on a small table or school desk.

Another advantage of such a frame is the ease with which the piece is laid aside without injury during the intervals of work. This is especially valuable where class problems are being conducted. It also permits of the work being done in any position—horizontal, inclined or upright.

When dyeing the material more than once the wax must be carefully mended after each dyeing, or soon the first spaces covered with the resist are lost or badly obscured. The material should always be dry before applying the wax.

COLORS PAINTED WITHOUT WAX OUTLINES

Some workers use pure beeswax. It does not break easily when worked in a warm dye-bath. It melts at a high temperature. Resin mixed with beeswax melts at a still higher temperature. There are special batik waxes that have all the desired qualities of toughness and resistance. These mixed waxes are similar to those used by industrial works in Java. Paraffin and beeswax are also used.

The best container for molten wax is a double boiler, the common kitchen utensil, as it is possible to keep the wax hot through a class period without having the heater in the class room. As means of heating, an electric toaster, gas plate, canned heat, etc., are suggested.

The wax must be applied hot. The brush, while waxing, should be kept hot to insure good penetration of the wax. To accomplish this, each time the brush is dipped into the molten wax it should be held there sufficiently long to remelt any wax that may have congealed in or on the brush.

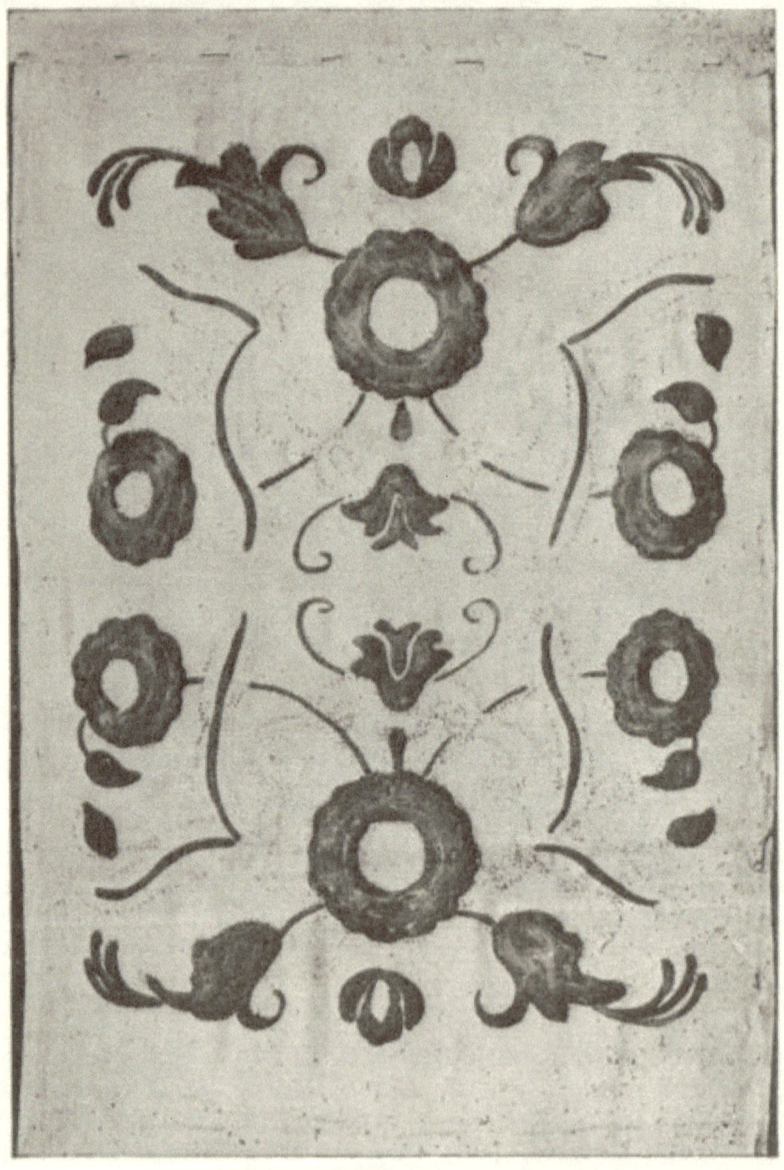

PART OF A DESIGN STOPPED OUT WITH WAX, READY FOR THE FIRST DYEING

To apply the wax, some use a tjanting. Others prefer the simpler method of a good sable or camel's hair brush. The brush gives a broader and more varied treatment. A broad brush is best for covering large surfaces. Brushes used for painting in oils or water colors are used for painting in wax and dyes.

Those who are interested further in the possibilities of the tjanting are referred to Pieter Mijer's excellent treatment of this subject.

Dyes suitable for pattern dyeing should not run or "bleed." Some use only primary colors. Others desire a more extended range. A good selection may include red, yellow, blue, orange, green, purple, brown and black.

The temperature of the dyes should be below the melting point of the wax. Care must also be used in dissolving dye. Granules in the dye-bath work havoc with an otherwise beautiful piece of dyeing. The dye should be filtered through a closely woven cloth. Prepared dyes insure safety, as the compounding and dissolving is done by formula.

After the last dyeing the fabric should be rinsed first in warm, then in cold water. Much of the wax is removed in the rinsing. The remainder of the wax is easily removed by ironing between layers of newspaper, followed if necessary by a bath of gasoline. If the piece is very large it should be finished by a professional cleaner.

There are different approved methods of pattern dyeing with wax resist, in the choice of which the craftsman must consider the conditions under which the work is to be done. We give in outline the steps of three methods:

I. Painting the decoration within waxed outlines, followed by one or more baths for the ground color. This is illustrated on pages 32, 33 and 34, where the following steps were taken:

1. A square of white china silk, clean and free of sizing, was stretched on a frame.

2. The main lines were sketched in with charcoal. The design was outlined in wax. The shapes were made small, as dye is liable to streak when painted over large areas.

3. The colors were mixed and used like water colors.

4. The small bell-shaped flowers were painted red, the pods yellow, the leaves green. These painted surfaces were then stopped out with wax.

5. Two gallons of warm water were softened and made into a soap suds. This solution was divided into two equal parts. The first part was used for wetting the fabric, and "soaping off" after dyeing. The second part was made into a brown dye-bath for the dipping.

II. Painting directly on the fabric without waxed outlines, and building up the ground color in one or more baths. The piece illustrated on page 35 was done as follows:

1. The design was drawn free hand upon the fabric, stretched in a frame.

2. The colors were painted directly. The tree was green, the bell-like flowers

orange, the dogs golden yellow. The brush strokes were very small.

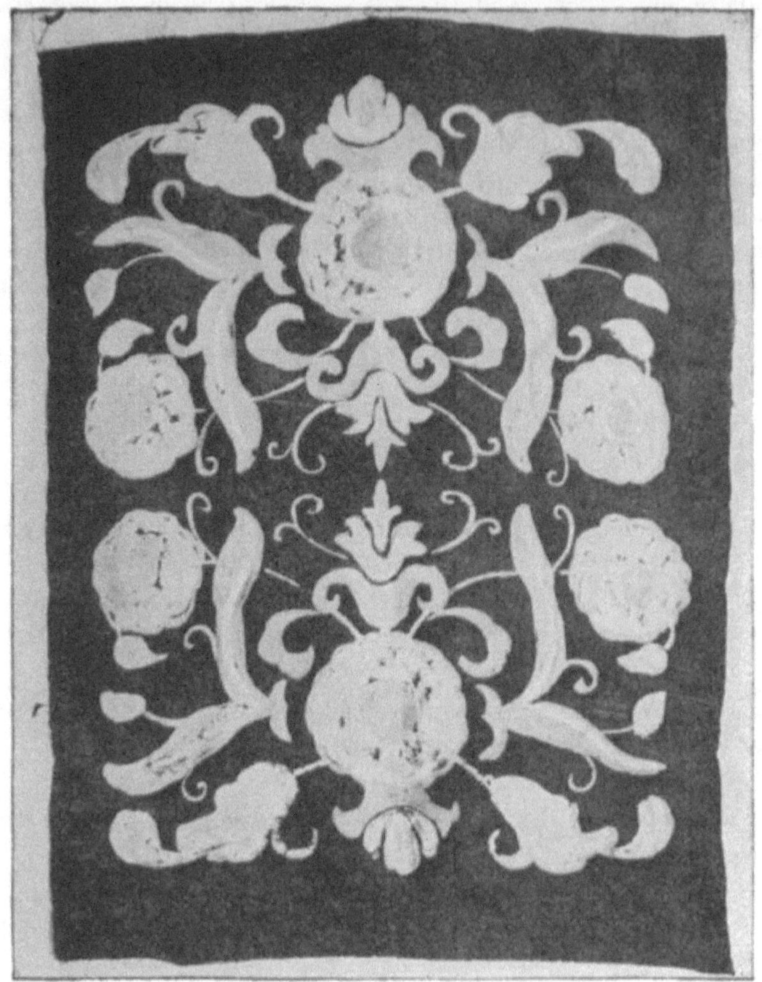

THE COMPLETED PATTERN

3. The colored shapes were carefully covered with wax.

4. The background was dyed a deep purple.

III. Building up the pattern by dyeing in successive baths, beginning with the lighter and passing to darker values, and before each dipping stopping out with wax the parts to be retained in the completed work. The piece illustrated on pages 36 and 38 was executed as follows:

1. The design was drawn on strong paper. This was then perforated, and the design pounced on the silk with powdered charcoal, using a stiff bristle brush and scrubbing the charcoal well through the holes.

2. The parts to remain white were stopped out by painting with wax.

3. The piece was dyed yellow, after which the design was again pounced.

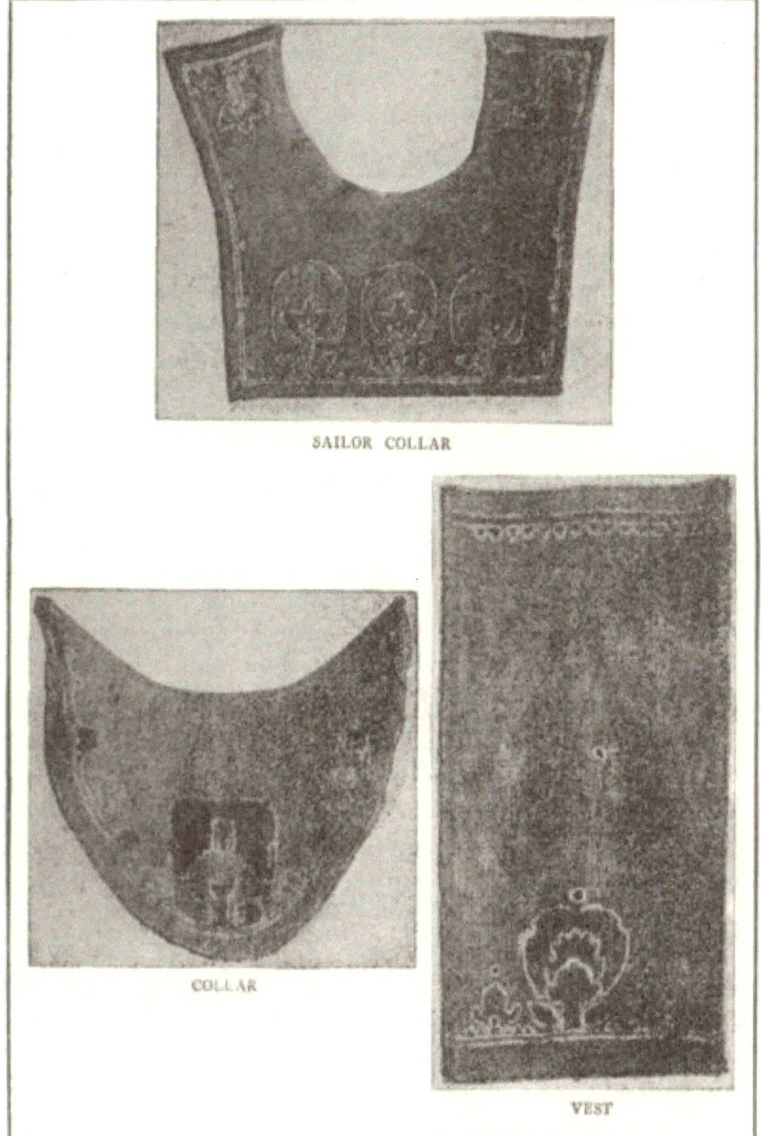

SAILOR COLLAR

COLLAR

VEST

SELECTED WORK OF ELEMENTARY HIGH SCHOOL CLASS

4. The parts to remain yellow were stopped out with wax.

5. The piece was dyed black.

In all these processes a small piece of the goods was carried completely through the dye-bath to test the color.

Some modifications of these processes are valuable. These follow, or are suggested by, practices of the Orient.

1. The design may be applied with blown stenciling.

2. Block printing and stick printing may be used and the color impressions covered with wax.

As concrete illustrations of textile decoration in schools we present some of the results of two class problems in high school, the one by a first and second year class, the other by third and fourth year pupils with a few who were posting.

First and Second Year Class. The pupils used the method of paper cutting to secure motives for their designs. Each pupil was supplied with enough white silk to make a collar, or a tie, also with color, wax and a frame upon which to stretch the silk. The method was that of outlining in wax, painting in color, and dipping for the ground color. The pupils were allowed to keep their work after paying for the materials. The illustrations on page 39 were chosen from the finished pieces.

The crepe-de-chene collar is 12 x 12 inches. The outside border and the largest shape at the point of the collar were old rose, the fan-like shape turquoise blue, the band and spottings at the side yellow. The inside border, buds and stem were blue and the alternating shapes yellow.

These colors were covered with wax and the collar dyed gray. It was then dipped in hot wax, carefully crackled and dipped in a dark gray bath. The wax was removed by ironing between layers of newspaper. Fine embroidery silk was dyed yellow and old rose for the stitchery that finished the edge of the collar.

The sailor collar was made of white china silk. The leaves of the design were painted green, the flowers rose color and the ground dyed a dark gray blue. The dye-bath was made of blue, black and purple. The collar was finished with yellow and old rose stitchery.

The pongee silk vest was designed for a tailored coat. The leaves and flowers were painted realistically. The ground was dyed blue and crackled in a darker blue bath. The edge was finished with dark red stitchery.

Third and Fourth Year Class. This work was conducted at a later time. In addition to more training, these pupils had for study many specimens of good batiks and standard illustrations of the same. The designs were made with reference to their fitness as batik designs.

The design units illustrated on page 46 were selected with reference to their adaptability to some form of all-over application.

The design for the book cover, also shown as an all-over pattern, page 43, the all-over pattern, page 41, and the scarf, page 42, were selected as the best work of this class.

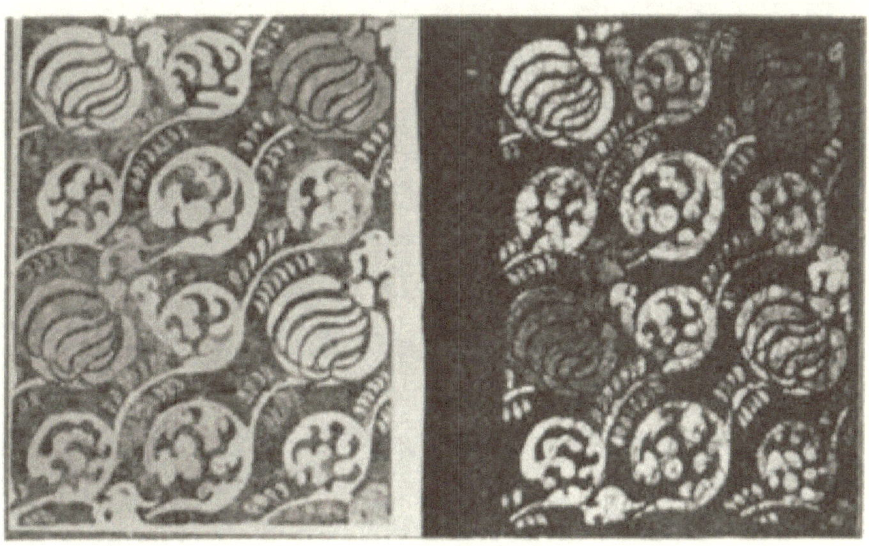

ALL-OVER PATTERN, ADVANCED HIGH SCHOOL

ALL-OVER PATTERN, ADVANCED HIGH SCHOOL

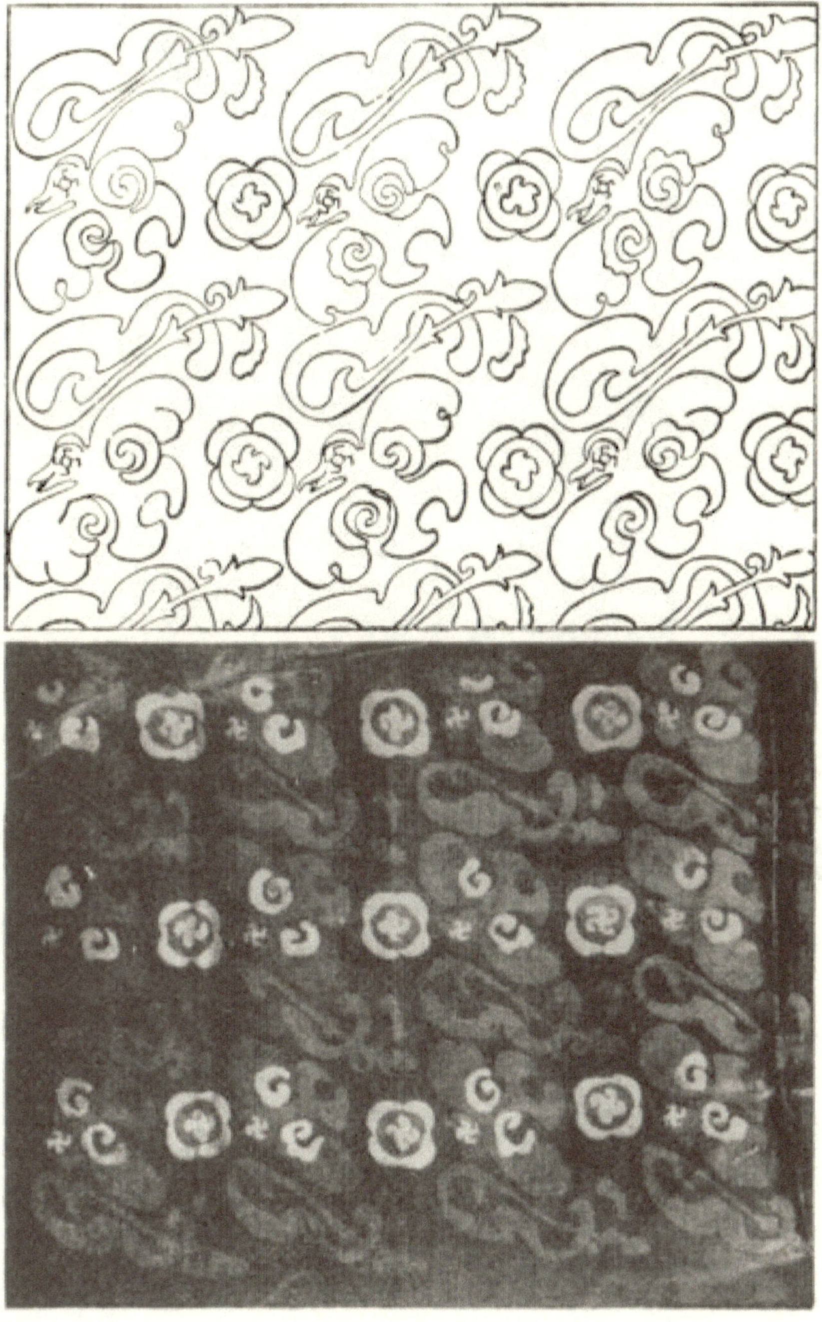

ALL-OVER PATTERN, ADVANCED HIGH SCHOOL

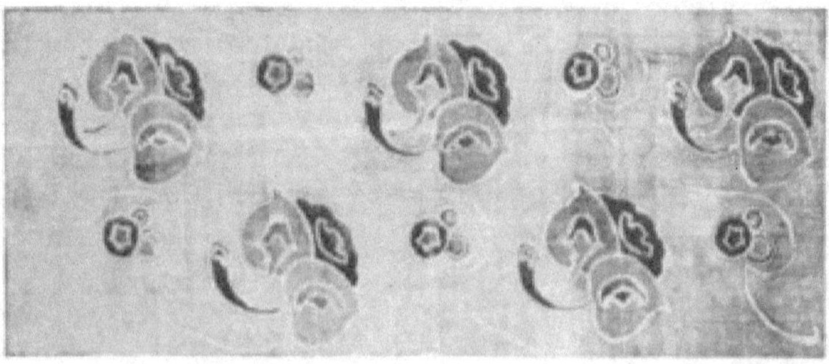

ALL-OVER PATTERNS, ADVANCED HIGH SCHOOL

A tracing of the all-over design, page 41, was first made and painted in water colors. The design was transferred to the silk by tracing. The colors of the decoration, following the copy in water color, were painted in without the use of wax outlines. The top units from left to right were blue, violet, yellow; second row, violet, blue, green, violet; third row, yellow, violet, blue; fourth row, violet, blue, green, violet. The stems were violet, the leaves yellow green. The background was dyed a rich brown.

The all-over design, page 42, was used for the end of a scarf. The silk was dyed yellow, parts of the decoration stopped out with wax, the flowers and body of the insect painted in red, the red stopped out with wax, and the background dyed brown. The scarf was finished with a fringe of orange silk.

The all-over design, page 43, was pounced on the silk after each dipping. The material was dyed yellow and the small spottings stopped out. The piece was dipped in a gray purple dye-bath. The resultant color was a grayed lavender. The larger shapes in the design were stopped out and the ground color dyed a deeper purple.

Two other examples of batiks from this class are illustrated:

1. The china silk blouse, page 44, with a yellow background and all-over pattern of white, blue and green shows a design that is suitable for yardage.

2. An all-over design, page 44, also suitable for yardage. The lavender flowers and leaves were painted inside waxed outlines. The spots were connected by flowing waxed outlines. The decoration was covered with wax and the ground color dyed a pale yellow gray.

The china silk handkerchief, page 47, is very interesting. The size is 17 x 17 inches with a one-inch hem. The area inside the hem was covered with wax, placed in a bath of cold water, and carefully crackled. It was then immersed in a blue dye-bath. After drying the same area was rewaxed, again crackled, and immersed in a red dye-bath. The result is very pleasing, a purple border with blue, red and purple crackle forming a delicate net work over the white center.

DESIGN UNITS FOR ALL-OVER PATTERNS

BATIKED HANDKERCHIEF

CHAPTER IV
BATIKS AND OTHER ILLUMINATED TEXTILES

APPLIED design has been the stabilizing factor in art education. It gives to art education a tangible reason for its place in the schools. It injects into every individual and class project the element of discipline that comes through being required to think in terms of definite mediums of expression.

The greatest emphasis, and for this reason perhaps the greatest success, has been its application in the field of costume designing and interior decoration. Batiks lay a just claim to having enriched this phase of art expression. A new creative and illuminating touch has been given to draperies, covers, cushions, scarfs, wall hangings, and costumes.

The following pages illustrate and explain a number of these illuminated objects.

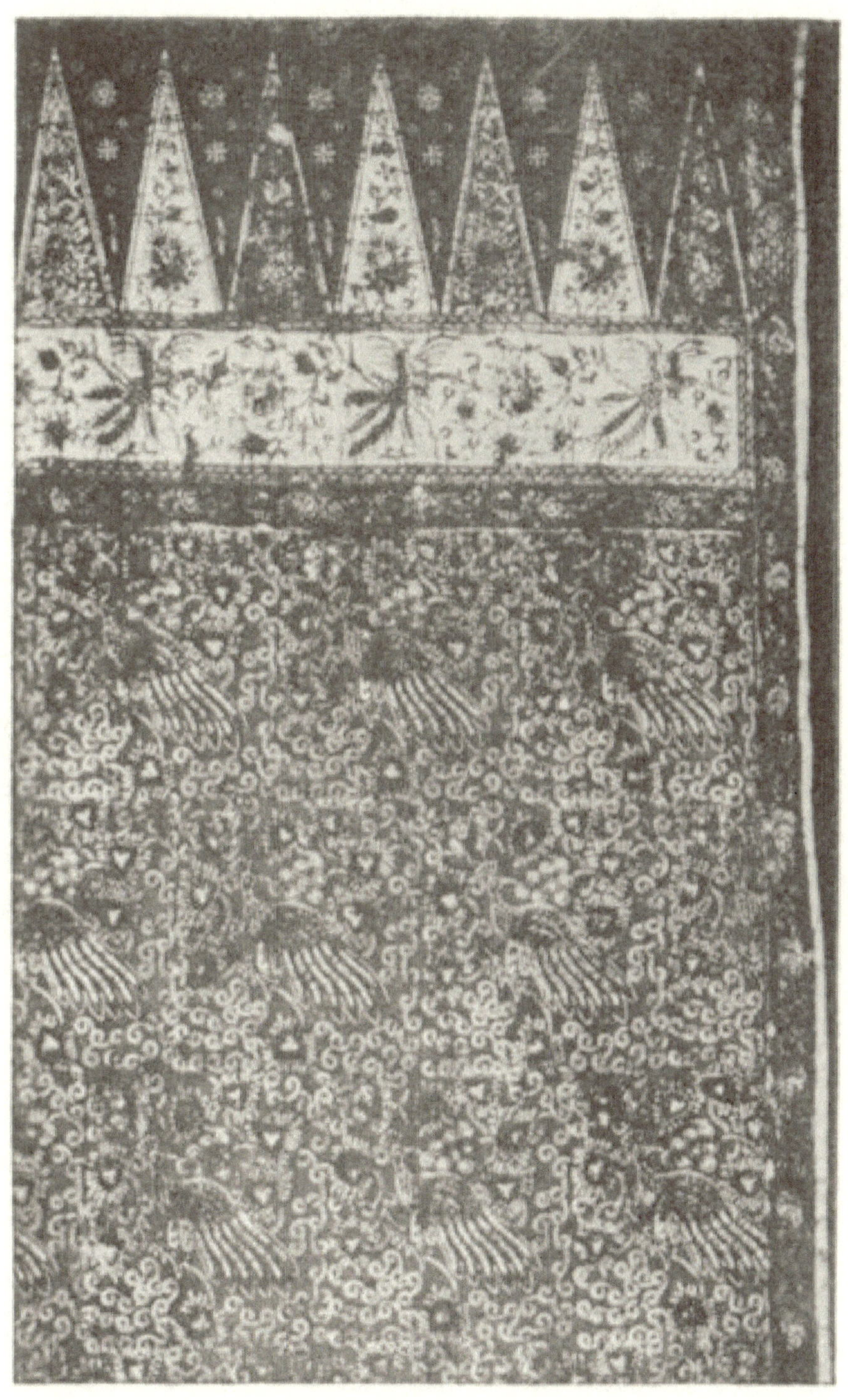

PORTION OF A JAVANESE SARONG

SARONGS

The sarong decorated with peacocks and vines is characteristic. The colors are red, blue and light yellow.

END PAPERS

The decoration of the end papers in this book is taken from the design of a very fine old sarong. The material is cotton. It has the quality and texture of the rarest batiks. The dyeing is vegetable indigo. Some of the units were perhaps applied with a tjap, but much of the waxing was done with single and double spouted tjantings. The ground color is a soft gray yellow.

SARONG DETAILS

The batik details shown on page 64 are all taken from old sarongs. The tjanting was used for all these patterns. They are excellent pieces of native craftsmanship.

The pattern on the left has a yellow gray background. The all-over dyeing is brown and the spottings dark red.

On the right the upper pattern has yellow gray in the background and brown decoration, the lower pattern has brown background and yellow gray decoration.

COSTUME JEWELRY

The band for this ornament, page 51, is made of several layers of georgette crepe picoted. It is ¾ inch wide and 1 yard long. The ornament, 1½ x 2³/₈ inches, was modeled from "petroplast," the modeling clay which sets without firing.

The silk was folded to four thicknesses. The wax was painted in a variety of interesting shapes on the white goods. Bands in red, yellow, green and orange were painted with dyes.

The petroplast was modeled smooth and the bird, flowers and pedestal were incised while the composition was still plastic. When dry it was dipped in black enamel. The outline of the bird was enameled in yellow and orange, the flowers painted in purple and blue, the pedestal in brown.

This adornment was planned to be worn as a necklace to brighten a dark costume.

COSTUME DECORATION

The costume decoration, page 30, was batiked on yellow taffeta silk.

The design was painted in with wax. The piece outside the decoration was covered with wax. The material was dipped in a dark brown bath and finished by ironing between layers of newspapers.

It is suitable for a vest or for millinery.

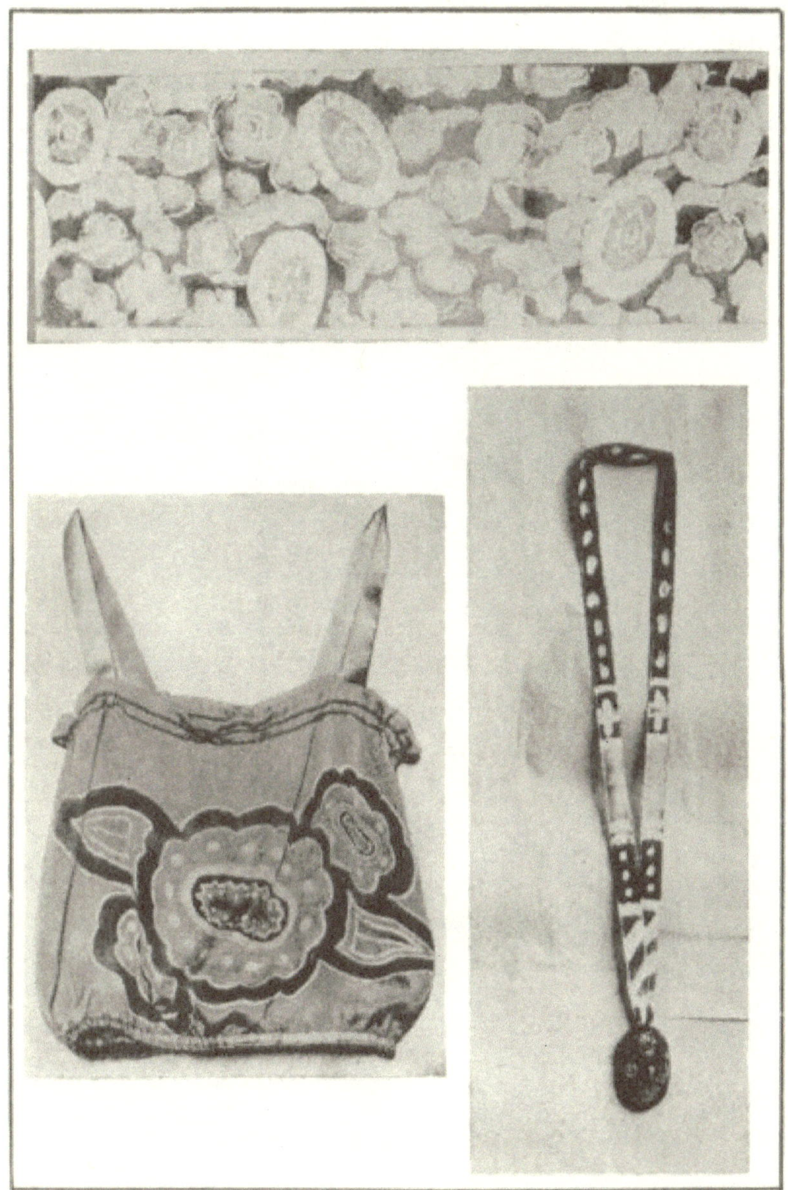

BATIKED RIBBON, CAMISOLE, AND COSTUME JEWELRY

BLOUSES

1. The blouse, page 55, with a rose design was made of white crepe-de-chene.

The outline of the decoration was waxed, and the roses and leaves painted conventionally. The borders and spaces were painted in wax. The border of the red was painted between waxed outlines.

The fabric was dyed blue, and finished with petroplast beads enameled in red.

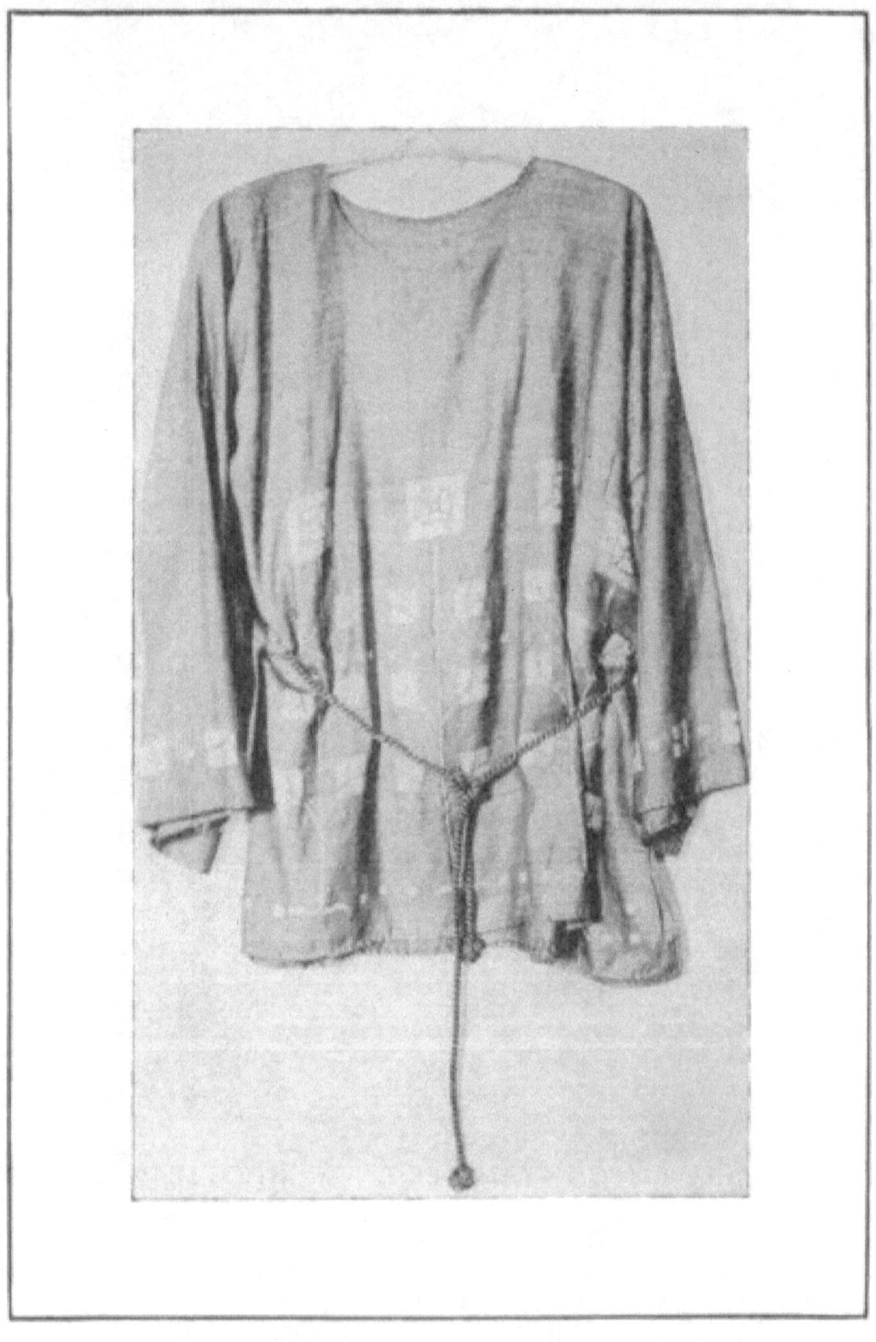

BATIKED BLOUSE

2. The detail of a georgette crepe blouse, page 58, with a dark background and all-over decoration in gold, is a suitable design for yardage. The piece was first dyed gold, and the pattern stopped out with wax. The dye-bath for the ground color was purple black.

3. The pongee silk blouse, page 52, is a good standard for service and artistic merit.

The leaves, stems and lower border decoration were painted in wax on the natural color of the cloth.

The piece was dyed blue, then the flowers and upper border were stopped out. A brown bath followed, giving as the final color a dark bronze. The blouse was belted with a bronze silk cord.

4. The crepe-de-chene blouse, page 54, has a rich green background with an after crackle in an orange bath.

The edges, sleeves and neck are decorated with a narrow orange and gray band.

Petroplast beads decorated to harmonize with the color of the silk, a brown cord girdle weighted with these ornaments, picoted edges, and stitchery of silk floss the same color as the cord finish a garment of great beauty and dignity.

SILK LINING

The crepe-de-chene lining illustrated on page 56 has a grayed yellow-green background. The flower motif has yellow, black and orange in the center, red and purple in the outer parts. The bud is red and purple. The stem and leaves are blue. These colors were painted within wax outlines.

There were eight yards of this lining. When rolling the waxed goods on the frame, a paper was rolled up with the material to prevent the wax from sticking.

The lining was used for a full length blue serge cape. After two dry cleanings, this garment was still fresh and beautiful.

CAMISOLE

1. The camisole, page 51, was made from a 14 x 36-inch piece of white crepe-de-chene. Half-inch purple ribbon, seven-eighths yard long, made the shoulder straps; a narrow purple ribbon gathered the top.

2. The design in yellow, brown and green was painted within wax outlines. The dyeing was in purple, the crackle penetrating the design.

3. The top was finished with double hemstitching.

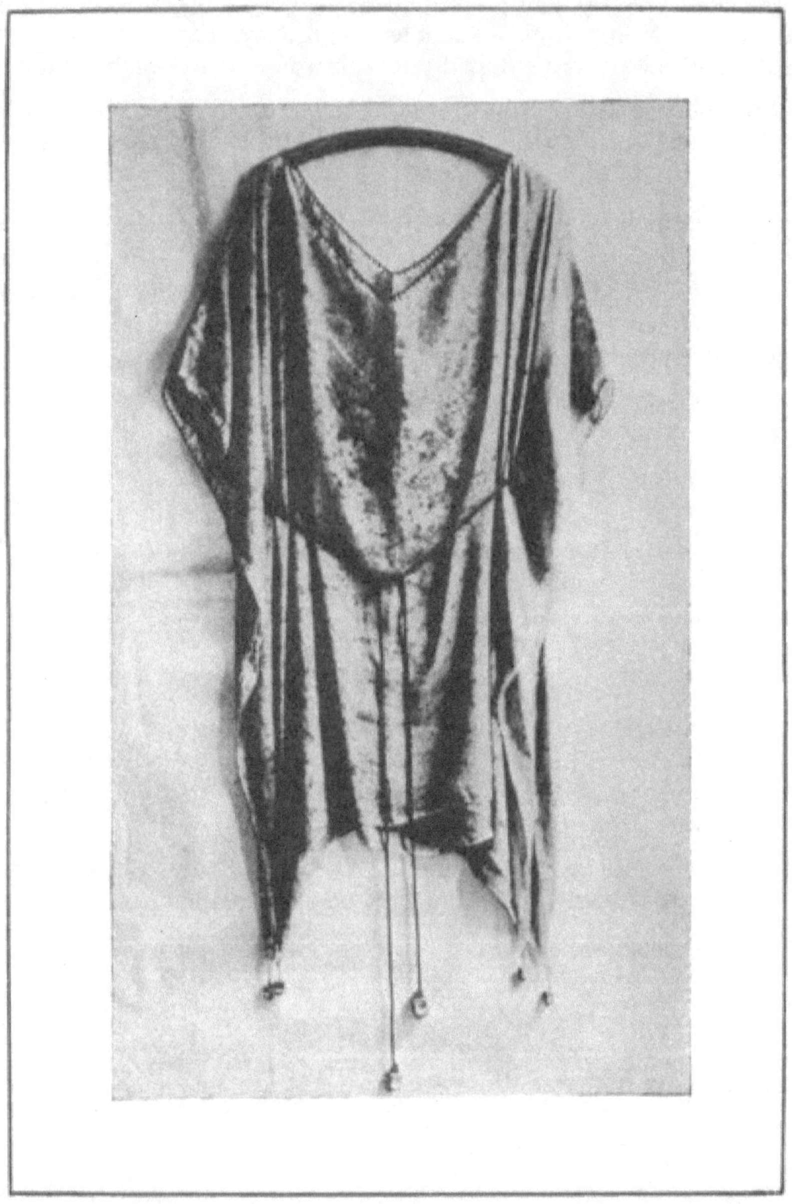

BATIKED BLOUSE WITH PETROPLAST ORNAMENTS

BATIKED RIBBON

The ribbon illustrated, page 51, was turquoise blue satin, 7½ x 36 inches.

The design was outlined and parts stopped out. The material was dyed in a blue dye-bath. The blue was stopped out in the flower shapes. The material was dyed in a yellow dye-bath. The leaves were stopped out. The material was dyed in a red dye-bath.

The decoration of the finished ribbon was turquoise blue, gray-blue and yellow-green. The background was dark olive green.

AN ILLUMINATED BLOUSE WITH PETROPLAST BEADS

A CAPE LINING

INTERIOR DECORATION

DOOR CURTAIN

The door curtain illustration, page 48, is a symbolic composition with a mystic wall and gate, and imaginary birds and a tree.

The color scheme is a black background, blue and purple tree, yellow and blue birds, a purple and orange fence and gate, and a foreground of blue, yellow and green.

The design was painted directly upon a good quality of silk, without guiding lines or waxed outlines. The painting was done very rapidly, perhaps in ten minutes.

The material was dipped several times, once in yellow, twice in red (more red was added to the dye-bath after the first red was exhausted), twice in the blue which was developed the same as the red, and at last back into the yellow. When the dyeing was completed the piece was thoroughly rinsed and the wax was removed.

The crackle caused through successive dyeings, the soft edges of the outlines and the blending of the background with the shapes freed the piece from the criticism often invited where colors are painted in large areas.

TABLE COVER

This design, page 59, (21 x 25 inches) consists of two conventional dogs adapted from the Chinese. The well-chosen colors are yellow and orange, with accents of black. The border decoration was painted in light green. Large and small spots suggest the use of the tjanting. The darkest values are reseda green.

The fabric was first dyed yellow. The dogs and spacing of borders were drawn in fine wax outlines. The dogs were painted orange, with small shapes of black for accents, and covered with wax. The material was then dipped in green dye, rinsed and dried.

The decoration for the border was drawn in wax, and the background for the dogs was also waxed.

In developing a pattern where so much drawing is needed, pains should be taken to retain the original outlines of the drawing. If the design is too much obscured after successive dippings, the drawing should again be transferred. The outline for the dogs and spacings for borders were saved by waxing. The green decoration on the border was not painted until after two dippings.

The crackle, tying the whole decoration, is even and adds beauty to the design.

The beauty of this batik lies in its fitness, its variety of line, its pleasing space relations and its good color scheme.

BATIK DETAIL FROM BLOUSE

ELEPHANT DECORATION

The elephant decoration illustrated on page 61 (27 x 25 inches) was done on white taffeta. The frame was made of two-inch basswood with a narrow gilt-edge moulding for a finish. The decoration on the frame was batiked.

The elephant, with its decoration and border, was outlined in wax.

BATIKED TABLE COVER

The vertical stripes numbered from left to right were: yellow (1-3-5-7-9); orange (2-6-10); magenta (4-8). These were painted in and covered with wax. The fabric was dipped in a dye-bath of grayed purple.

The design on the frame was painted in wax and the colors in the design reproduced from the colors in the silk. Most of the wax was removed with a knife and the balance with a gasoline wash. It was afterwards finished with a coating of wax.

This wall hanging has a few spots where the treatment was not thorough. The red stripe under the elephant's head shows unintentional breaking in the wax. Too much blue crept into many places. It cannot be emphasized too many times—before painting over the colors with wax, the colors must be dry.

This work illustrates the success of painting in rather large surfaces of color without streaks appearing and harmonizing the whole by tying together with crackle. The design of the elephant and the outside border are unusually meritorious.

"A TABLE BEFORE ME"

This decoration was drawn on glazed paper and pounced on white china silk, 40 x 72 inches. There was no painting of colors, the process being one of dippings only.

The design was outlined in wax. The small spottings, border lines and markings in the vine were stopped out, and the piece was dipped in a yellow dye-bath.

Through each dipping a dye record was kept by carrying a small piece of the goods through the dye-bath. After each dyeing the wax was carefully mended.

The bell-like flowers in bands or borders, the flowers at the foot of the vine, the body, wing, tail and lower part of the bird's legs, tendrils, dragon fly and border were stopped out, and the piece dyed orange.

The remaining bands and shapes in the flowers, inside and outside border, and tendrils were stopped out and the next dipping was blue. The background and remaining shapes were a lovely warm gray lavender.

Part of the leaves, head of the bird, upper part of the bird's legs, shapes in the foreground, and roots of the vine were stopped out. The next dyeing was blue.

The vine, remaining leaves, tendrils, the remainder of the foreground and spaces that were needed to fill in were drawn in wax.

The wax was removed from the wing and the tail of the bird and the batik dipped in a dye-bath of deep blue.

The color range in this piece includes red-orange, yellow, blue, turquoise, two shades of lavender, green and sparkles of white broken by every color, on a gray-blue background.

The work on this batik extended over a period of two weeks.

"THE CAPTURE"

The frontispiece is worthy of special study.

The material was white pussy willow silk, 40 x 72 inches.

A sketch of the design, 6½ x 10 inches, was made in water colors.

A WALL HANGING WITH BATIKED FRAME

"A TABLE BEFORE ME," BY IDA STRAWN BAKER

The fabric was freed from sizing and dyed a pale yellow.

It was then stretched in a frame and the three "thunder birds," the clouds, and a few flowers in the foreground were painted in wax. The bills, eyes and legs of the birds were painted in with orange dye.

The roadway, parts of the rocks, drapery on the Indian maiden, some of her decoration, and parts of the foliage, were painted directly on the silk with yellow or orange dye.

The remaining foliage, more decoration worn by the maiden, the grass, leaves on the flowers and the stems were painted green.

These shapes were stopped out with wax. Much painting in of shapes was done with wax. This gave a finish and jewel-like quality to the work as it progressed.

Before the material was dyed it was soaked in warm water the same temperature as the dye-bath. The piece was then dyed in a bath of blue. It was worked constantly for about ten minutes. It was removed from the dye and rinsed in clear warm water.

After rinsing, the material was placed flat between layers of bath towels and much of the moisture removed. The drying was finished by hanging over a waxed line.

The sky and the blue of the border were next stopped out, leaving for the next bath the pony, the remainder of the Indian maiden, the tree trunks and other shapes in the foreground.

The frame was placed in an upright position after the custom of Javanese workers. While waxing, the light shone through and every uncovered spot was easily seen. A medium sized soft brush was used for stopping out the large spaces.

Great care was taken to drain the excess wax from the brush. This is more necessary when the work is erect, as it prevents the wax from running down the goods.

The third dye-bath was prepared with red and a little yellow. A piece of the fabric dyed with the last dipping was dyed in this bath to test the color. The material when dyed in this bath was a rich, red-purple.

After partly drying with bath towels the piece was stretched on the frame to finish drying.

When thoroughly dry the entire surface was waxed except the mane and tail of the horse, the hair of the maiden, a few of the jewels, some details in the foreground, and the ground of the border.

All the broken places in the wax were carefully mended for the final dipping. The colors for the bath were dark green and black. The piece was finished by rinsing in warm water, then in cold, and finally by a gasoline bath.

The work extended over a period of two weeks.

It is a finished piece, rare and beautiful in its illumination.

DETAILS FROM OLD SARONGS

CHAPTER V
DYEING FOR PLAYS AND PAGEANTS

THE play bases its claim in the school curriculum on the very essence of human nature. The art of being someone or something else in thought and action under a setting of conditions and through a flow of events is practiced by all of us. It is the eternal expression of playful and imitative childhood, and, though restraints enter with maturity, it never leaves us. Witness the audience we give to the stage.

This has been recognized in the study of the play in literature and in the production of the school play. The application of the art training of the school in giving the play its setting and costumes is of the greatest value. The life of a school finds expression, through co-operation of all departments, in its own community theater.

Dyeing is an important consideration in a dramatic production. Colorful costumes and properties have a large part in making a play.

MINIATURE STAGES, PLAIN AND DECORATED BY CHILDREN

STAGE SCENES IN MINIATURE

The possibilities of continuous play without scene shifting, by drawing un-obtrusive curtains alternately to the right and to the left—creating atmosphere by the merest suggestion—is simple when dyes and dyeing enter into the plans of the setting. The old heavy painted scenery is not a part of the new drama.

The ground cloth and colored lights also offer opportunities for the service of the dyer.

Costumes are more easily created when soft old materials are dyed, and it re-quires but little experience to discover how the beauty and effectiveness of a play are enhanced thereby.

The proscenium arch takes its place in the illusion, when the imagination is stimulated by color decoration.

There should be an intimate co-operation between the community of little theater and craft workers.

The relation of the little theater to those who do handicraft is stated by Mr. George Somnes, Director of the Little Theater of Indianapolis, as follows:

"Too much stress cannot be laid upon the importance of all-over dyeing, batiks, and other pattern dyeing, and their application in the work of the little theater.

"Preeminently the little theater stands for the giving of the theater back to the artist, be he producer, musician, scene designer, costume designer, dancer or author. There is the endeavor to establish each little theater group as a means of community expression. The use of color in its relation to the play and lights, as scenery and in costumes, is so obvious and necessary that it needs scarcely more than mention. As experimentation is necessary and desirable, there must be at the bottom an actual foundation and knowledge upon which to experiment and build.

"School plays and pageants could be improved many hundred percent if the knowledge of color and its application were made more general. Not only would children be taught that green and red go together, but they would be taught just *what* greens and reds form the various combinations—they could find out under what lights certain colors react best.

"Give us more artists and craftsmen and we will have a real theater; give us local artists and craftsmen and we will have a Community Theater."

In the following item from "The Workshop," the magazine issued by the Little Theater Society of Indiana, the editor writes to the community of the dyed costumes used in "Dierdre of the Sorrows."

"The Little Theater Society feels it very significant that they are able to call attention to the use of color in the present production and to mention that its application in this play is the work of local artists. The Waldcraft Studios have generously given time, service and experience to help make this production complete. Does not that sound hopeful for our development, and by example, are there not more people in other fields who can give their time, knowledge and experience to the development of something which when it is completed as an institution will belong to you?"

The illustrations shown in this chapter are, (1) a plain miniature stage constructed of pasteboard and upon which the study of the decoration for a school play may well begin, (2) two stages that have been thus decorated, (3) two scenes in a play with miniature jointed dolls wearing real dyed costumes made by children, (4) several children at work designing and constructing for plays, (5) a group of scenes from a play given in a backyard, for which the costumes were especially dyed, (6) another miniature stage made of wood, shown plain and decorated with dyed hangings for a play, and (7) some character parts from the Little Theater of Indianapolis, for which special dyeing was done.

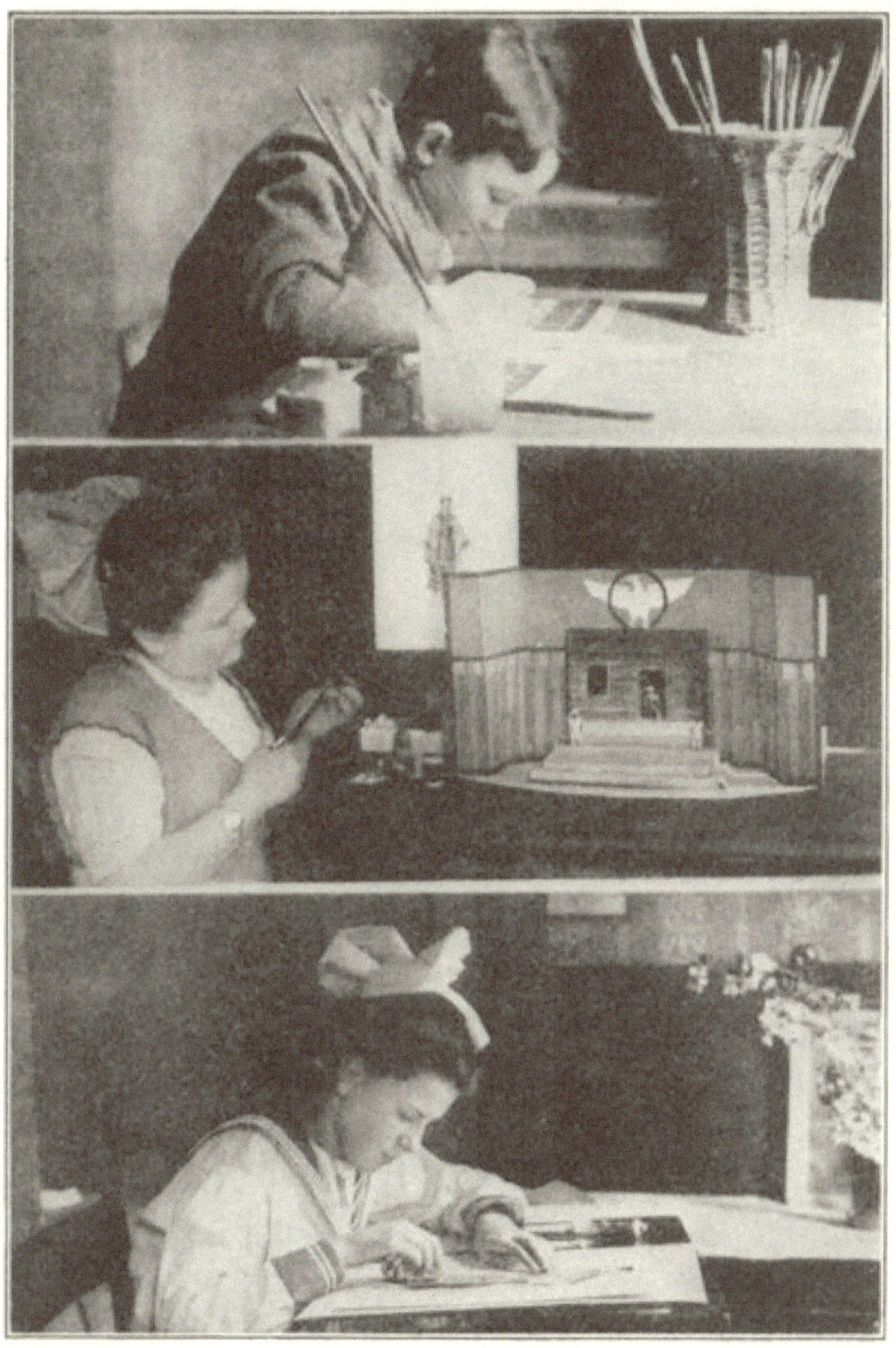

MINIATURE STAGECRAFT

MINIATURE STAGE, PLAIN AND DRAPED WITH BATIKED HANGINGS

The miniature pasteboard stages, page 66, were decorated with opaque water colors by school children. These illustrate the preliminary step in decorating a stage with dyed textiles. They would reproduce in batiks.

The first decorated stage is planned to play "Treasure Island." The decoration over the proscenium arch is "The little ship that is headed south-west," and the border,

> "Fifteen men on a dead man's chest,
> Yo-ho-ho and a bottle of rum."

The background colors are blue and black, the ship white and the fifteen men red and white.

The other stage is planned for a patriotic entertainment. The colors for this occasion are conventional.

The miniature stage in wood (page 70) and the ensemble pictured suggests dyeing of stage properties.

The proscenium arch of this little stage was decorated for the study of the play "Restoring the Mourners." The dramatic story tells of the exile of the Miami Indians from Indiana to Kansas. When this event took place there were seventeen states in the Union. The Indians called these states the "Seventeen Fires" (Council Fires). These "fires" were treated symbolically in the border at the top of the proscenium arch.

The fires, realistic in color, were painted in and stopped out with wax. The panels were dyed blue. The spaces back of the fires and the council were stopped out with wax and the whole dyed a deep purple. This stage construction is suitable for the end of a room or hall where there is no balcony or for out-of-doors.

The curtain, seen through the proscenium arch and enlarged on page 74, is an interesting batik dyed in values of red, blue and purple.

The decoration was painted realistically on the white silk and covered with wax.

The bottom of the piece for about four or five inches was kept in the dye-bath until most of the color was exhausted. A small amount of red was added to the bath and little by little the material was immersed in the bath until about two-thirds of the goods were dyed.

The top of the material was dyed blue in like manner.

The bottom is a brilliant red, the top a bright blue and the center different values of purple and pale lavender.

The pictures of Mr. George Somnes and Mrs. Eugene Fife as Naisi and Dierdre, in "Dierdre of the Sorrows," page 73, illustrate some of the hand-dyed costumes for this play.

SCENES FROM AN OUT-OF-DOOR PLAY

Mrs. Fife's cloak was a beautiful clear blue; her dress a dark red; the tie-dyed veil a deep purple; the design an intense yellow-gold.

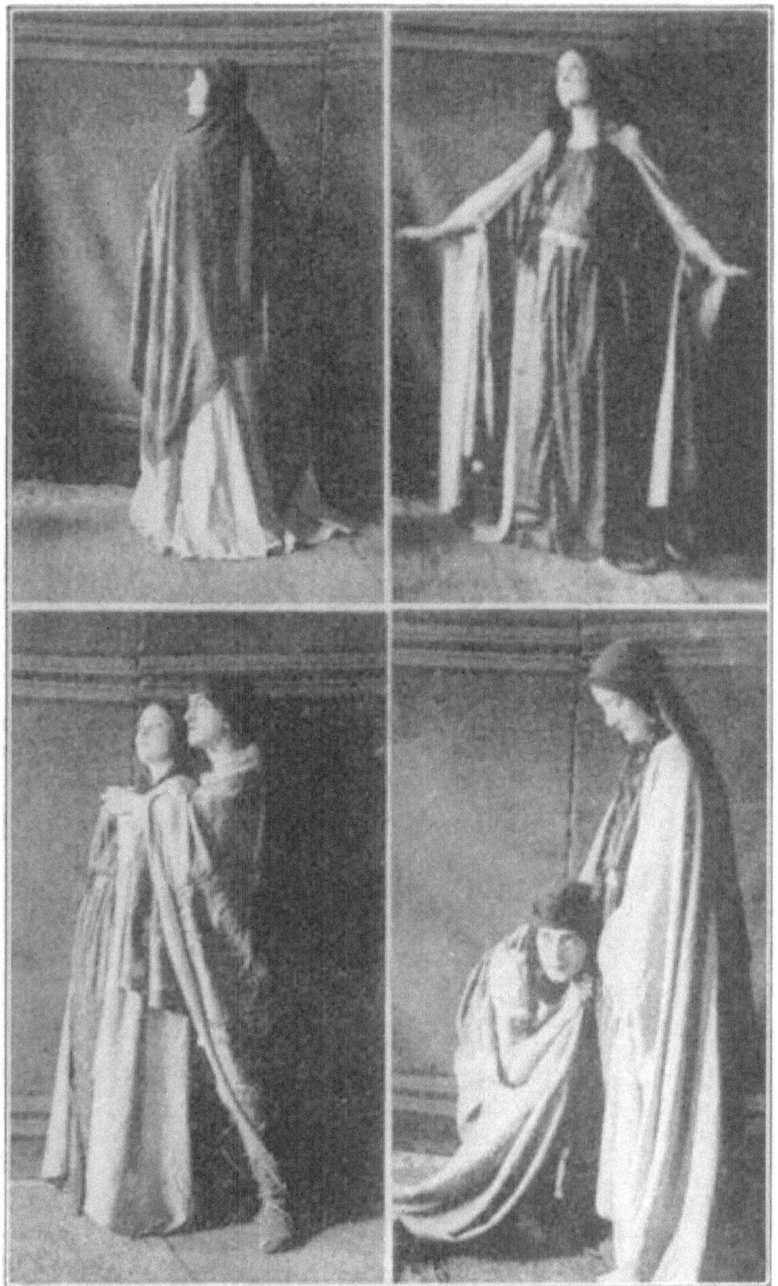

HAND DYED COSTUMES FROM THE LITTLE THEATER

There was no attempt to show batik in the decoration. The wax resist was the easiest means of decorating the costume.

Mr. Somnes' cloak was a purple gray with symbolic designs painted in wax. His boots were dyed brown.

These costumes were made of old material. All of the costumes were dyed to suggest contact with the elements.

A SCENE CURTAIN

CHAPTER VI
TIE-DYED WORK

THIS beautiful and fascinating art of textile decoration, applied to draperies and articles of dress, has been practiced in many countries for centuries. Old pieces have been found in South America, in Peru and Bolivia. In the Philippines and in provinces of India the work may still be seen, the art having been handed down from generations unknown.

The essential process consists in dyeing the cloth in a dye-bath after having wound parts of it more or less tightly with string or cord, which serves as a resist to prevent the color from reaching those parts of the fabric. The result is a white or, if the cloth has been previously dyed, a light colored pattern on a darker background.

The method is capable of more elaborate work. There may be several dyeings, beginning with lighter colors and passing to those of darker values, and between the dyeings additional tying or untying or both.

PORTION OF A CHUNDRI SHOWING TIE-DYED WORK DONE IN INDIA

For example, a cloth is dyed light gray, then a pattern tied into it, after which it is put through a light blue dye-bath. This gives a light gray design upon a grayed blue background. But suppose now that a part only of the tying is removed, some additional tying done in the grayed blue field, and a third dye-bath used, this time a light red. The background becomes a grayed purple and in the design are gray, grayed blue and grayed red.

There may be a great variety of designs, depending upon the manner of tying the individual unit and the spacing of these units with relation to each other.

The Oriental work is characterized by very small individual ties and the arrangement of many of these into some geometrical or pictorial pattern. The grouping of these little ties accurately and uniformly into lines and design clusters challenges wonder and admiration. But even with the dexterity acquired by these people the process is slow and laborious.

The illustration (page 76) shows a piece of tie-dyed work from India. The material is cotton. Careful examination shows it to have been done in the following manner: The cloth, which is very thin, was folded to form four thicknesses. Then at each point where a tie was desired the four thicknesses were pressed or drawn up and wound very tightly with string, the very tip of the fabric being left exposed to take the dye like the background. After dyeing and removing the ties the cloth was unfolded, showing the four repeats. The upper left quadrant was uppermost in the tying, and shows the dark centers very distinctly. Then came in order the upper right showing small dark centers, the lower right showing few dark centers, and the lower left showing none at all.

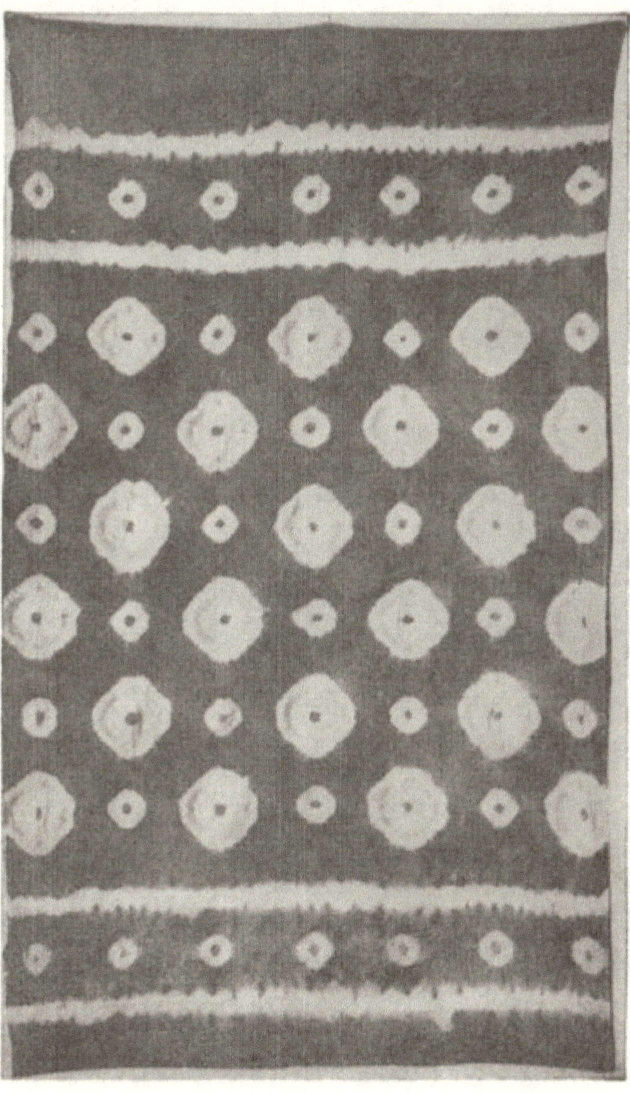

A TIE-DYED PATTERN BY HIGH SCHOOL PUPIL

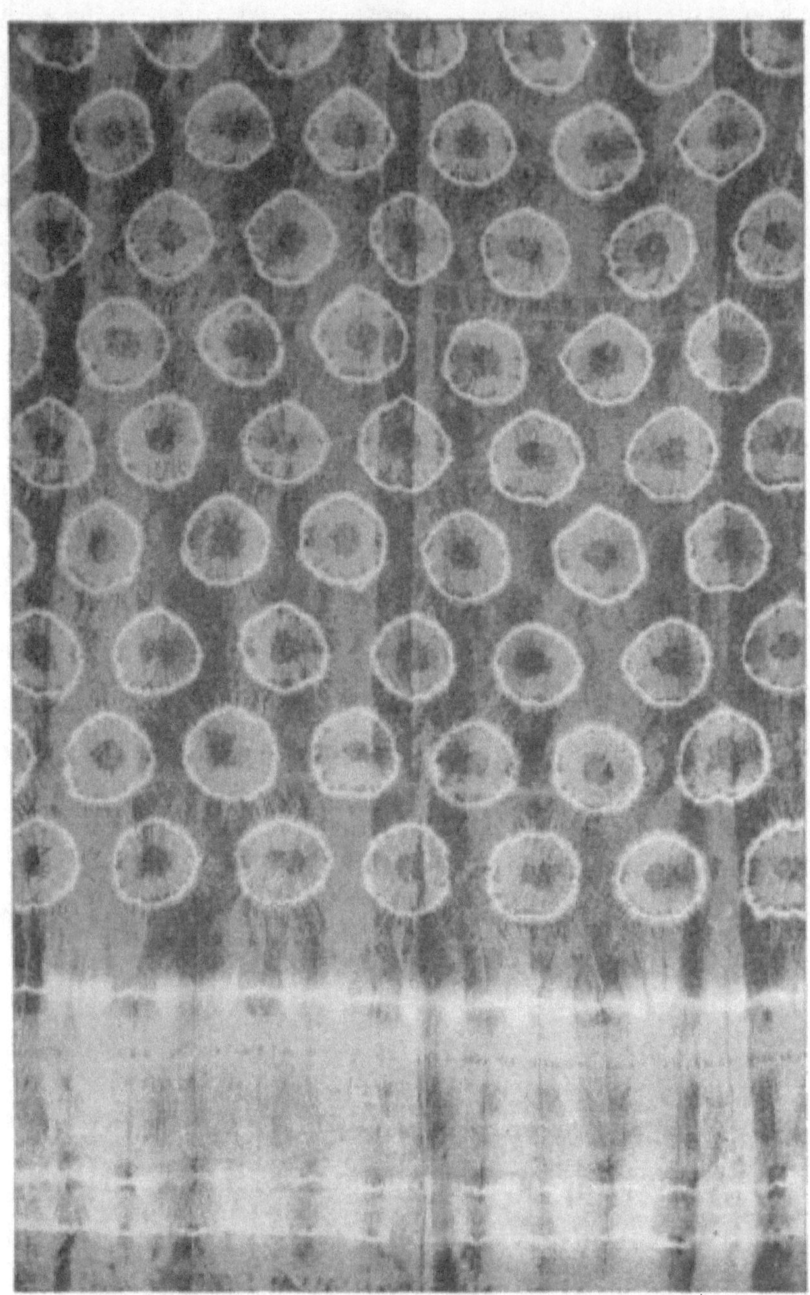

PORTION OF A TIE-DYED SILK SCARF

As with other crafts that have come to us from the East, we have not chosen to imitate their marvelous perfections of detail. It has rather been to our liking to work out space and color adjustments in a manner more in keeping with our national temperament. And it is not without its measure of success in artistic and pleasing results.

The illustration on page 77 is the work of a school boy. The material was cotton, dyed old rose before the tying was done. After the tying it was dyed deep blue. The space relations are very good.

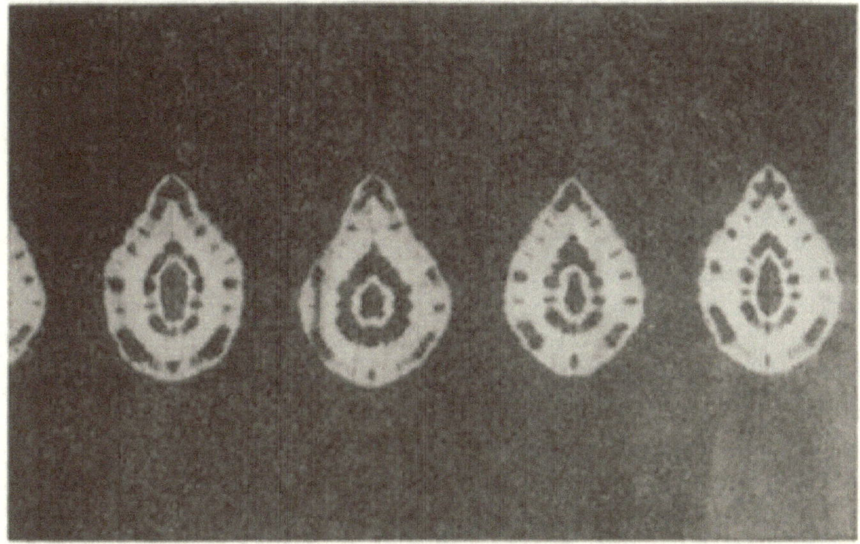

A TIE-DYED BORDER

PORTION OF A TIE-DYED SCARF

The work upon such a piece should proceed in the following manner. First the cloth should be prepared for dyeing in the manner indicated in the chapter on dyeing. The centers of the ties should next be located. Sometimes the cloth is merely gathered at each center and tied, but with larger patterns it is often folded in some definite way. The border in this piece was made by gathering across the entire piece and tying.

If the tying is very tight the outlines will be sharp. With a little looseness in the ties the color will creep in, the results of which are often very beautiful. A tie that is too loose, however, is in danger either of coming off in the dye-bath, or it may allow the color to penetrate to the extent of destroying the design.

Too prolonged treatment in the dye-bath, or dyeing at too high a temperature, may cause too much penetration of color into the tied spaces.

On page 78 is shown a portion of a silk scarf. In this case the white cloth was gathered at the respective centers, without any definite plan of folding, and tied rather tightly with a few winds of string about an inch or more from the center. The piece was then dyed a soft gray yellow. Then more winding was done so as to leave only the tips exposed. The next dye-bath was a soft blue somewhat stronger than the yellow. The color qualities are beautiful. The border shows the penetration of the blue color in a very happy manner.

The border design on page 79 shows the result of a definite manner of folding the cloth before tying.

The portion of a scarf illustrated on page 79 shows one large pattern beginning at the center of the scarf. The scarf was gathered or folded from the center and tied at intervals. The color is delicate old rose, especially beautiful for evening wear.

Sometimes small objects, such as marbles or glass beads, are placed at the center of the tied spots and the cloth tied around them.

A very interesting development of tie-dyed work and one which greatly increases the variety of designs is what we may term stick tying, *i.e.,* tying over sticks.

The sticks for this purpose are those commonly used by school children in stick printing. These are sold by all the leading school art supply houses. These sticks are treated so they will not absorb color, which makes them especially suitable for tie-dyed work. They are of different shapes, squares, circles, triangles, oblongs, etc. On these shapes the cloth may be folded in different ways, giving an element of geometrical symmetry, which, however, is always softened in the dye-bath as the color makes its little incursions into the tied spots.

Stick tying is not only a good craft problem but also splendid for the school room for both boys and girls.

It is best to lay out the design on the cloth by stick printing with a very light tint of the color to be used in the first dyeing, and using, of course, the end of the stick over which the cloth is to be tied. This insures a proper direction of the axes of the tied spots.

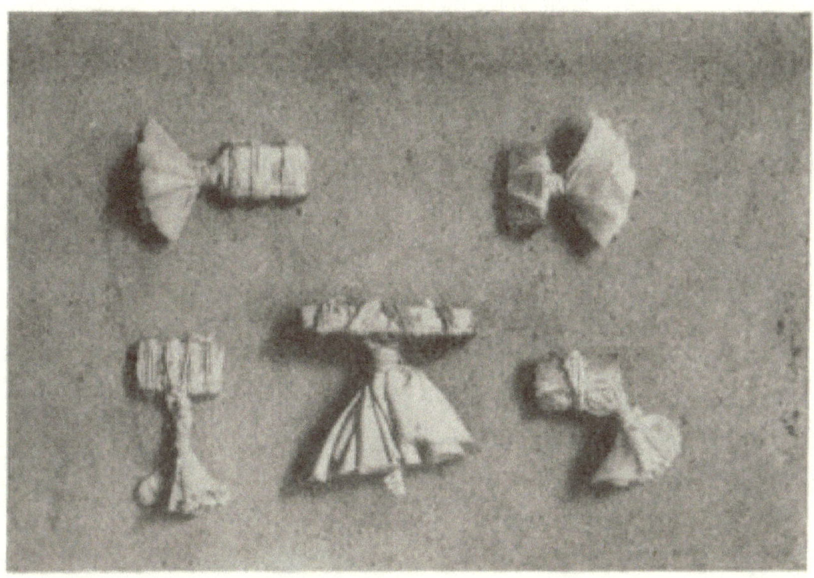

EXAMPLES OF STICK TYING

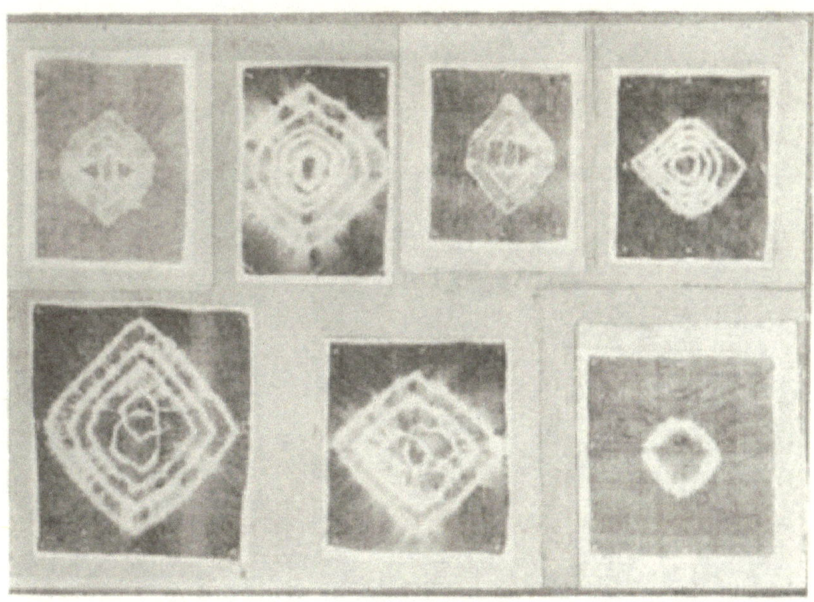

STICK TIED PATTERNS

On page 81 are shown a number of tyings over the different sticks, and also some dyed spots resulting from tying in several ways. Any school boy can devise other stick ties, and he will be delighted with some of the effects produced by his inventions.

We also show (page 82) a silk scarf tied over sticks, with a border at each end, ready for the dye-bath. On page 83 is this same scarf after dyeing. The work was carried out in the following manner: The stick used was a flat oblong one-eighth inch thick, five-eighths inch wide and one inch long. The cloth was stick printed with light yellow to locate the centers for the ties. The end of the stick was placed at the center, the cloth folded equally on the two sides, and the tying done as shown on the first stick (page 81).

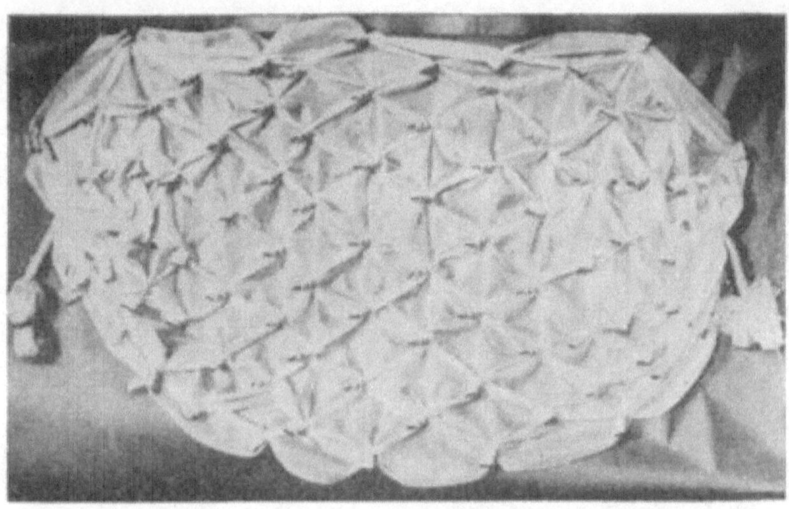

A PIECE OF STICK TYING READY FOR THE DYE-BATH

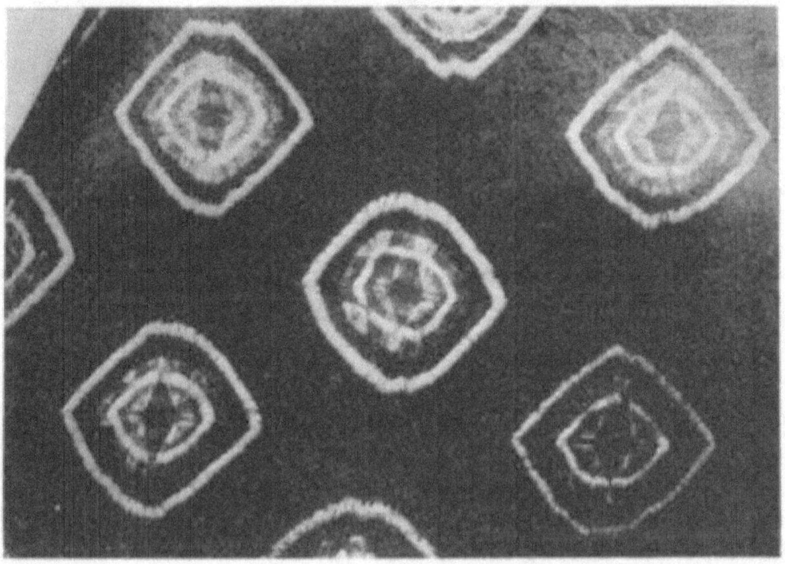

UNITS OF THE PATTERN FROM THE ABOVE TYING

The entire scarf was dipped in warm water before dyeing. This conformed to our directions for dyeing and also caused the ties to tighten. The piece was first dyed yellow, then without any change in the tying it was dyed green.

A SILK DRAPERY DECORATED BY STICK TYING

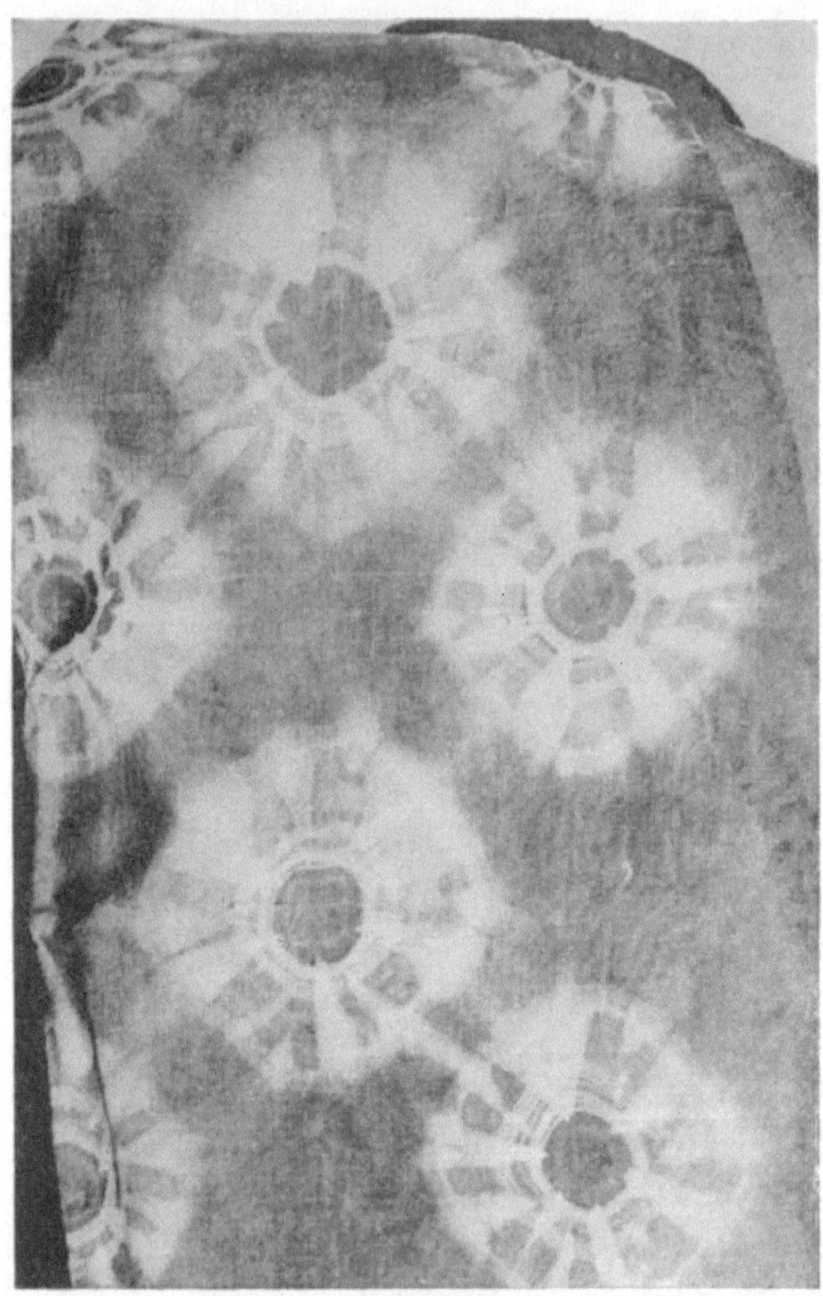

A STICK-TIED LINING FOR JACKET

After a thorough rinsing the two yellow green bands around the stick were protected by additional tying and the upper and lower ties removed, exposing two white bands. Then followed a red dyeing, another rinsing, the removal of all ties, and a final dyeing in a very dilute golden yellow.

The result is a ground color of rich, beautiful brown. In the tied spots are bands of gold, of orange-red, of yellow-green and of brown, also a brown center. Along the edges of these bands the colors have crept in, one here and another there, to produce a beautiful iridescence. The same colors are repeated in the borders.

The lining of the jacket, page 84, is a beautiful piece of stick tying on pongee silk. The colors here are yellow, green and grayed purple, as well as the original color of the pongee. These were three dye-baths, yellow, blue and red.

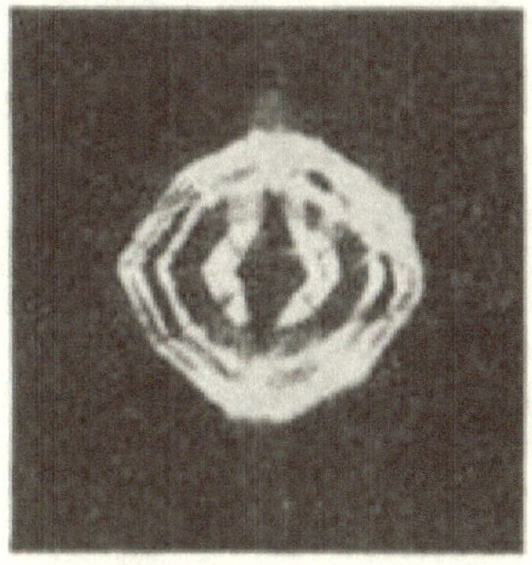

CHAPTER VII

STICK PRINTING, BLOCK PRINTING AND STEN-CIL DYEING

IT has been seen how versatile the batik method is as a means of illuminating fabrics, also how design is the controlling element in all good batik work. In both the space and color relations the batik worker has control of the entire surface subject only to the limitations imposed by the mediums in which he is working.

It follows that a knowledge of the principles of design must underlie good batik work as well as a knowledge of dyes.

In taking up the other ways in which school children are using dyes, it is well to place emphasis upon the design elements involved. All dyeing as done by craftsmen and in the schools involves design. Even all-over dyeing is carried out with the idea of the dyed piece becoming a part of some larger whole.

The earliest use of dyes in the schools is in stick printing, and here begin the first lessons in pattern dyeing.

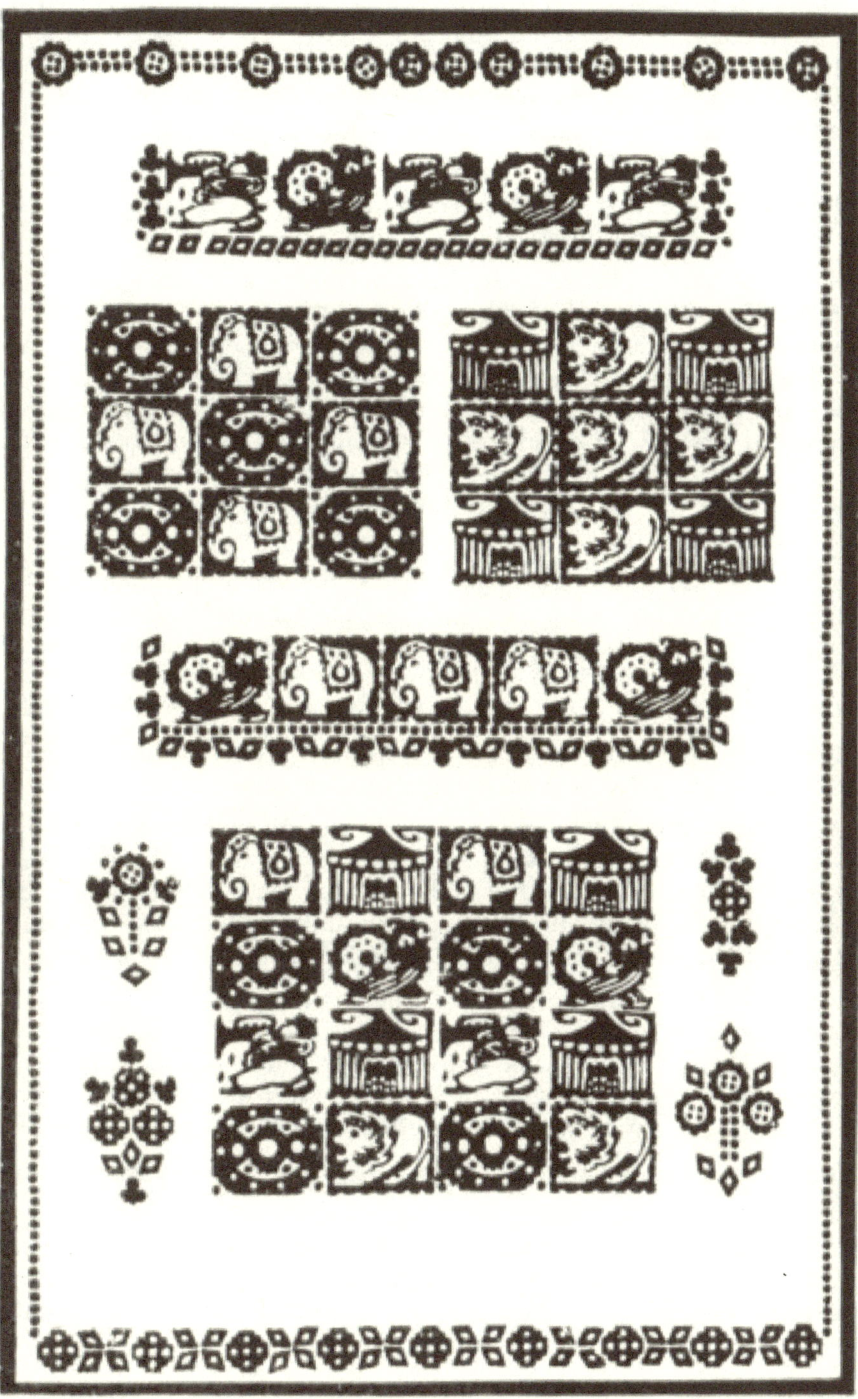

SUGGESTED USE OF BLOCK PRINTING FOR END PAPER

All shapes used in design resolve themselves into certain recognized types. These type shapes are the square, oblong, triangle, circle, ellipse and oval. There are also standards of color that have become associated with these types. They are red, yellow, blue, orange, green and violet. These shapes and colors are taught universally by teachers who train children in the elementary concepts of design.

It is the adjustment of these shapes and colors in space that constitutes design. It is the application of these shapes and colors to definite materials for definite uses in the child's life that constitutes applied design.

When the child prints a square on his paper it is a real square and good in color. The next one will be a real duplicate, both in shape and color. The problem is where to put the duplicate. That is the essence of design, and both teacher and pupil are ready to take hold of it. There is time for discussion and drill. Results must follow. The child begins to sense and appreciate standards and to love accuracy, neatness and orderliness. His interest is sustained and his powers strengthened through satisfactory accomplishment. He plans, invents, and executes, acquires independence of thought and expression, and designs in accordance with his imagination and experience.

Very early in the child's training, while the stick printing is unfolding the elements of design to him, he applies his designs to enrich his construction work. It is the time for the child to begin through concrete efforts to get rooted into his thinking that designs are made to be applied and that everything which contributes to his comfort, happiness and well-being exists because a design has been applied.

Then is also the time for the child to see some printed textiles in which the pattern is geometrical like his stick printing.

After the child has had sufficient experience with type shapes, he may add block printing. With the knowledge and experience gained through the use of sticks, he is enabled to modify the standard shapes. A wood block veneered with linoleum that can be easily cut with a sharp knife into any form desired, and which maintains a rigid printing surface, brings this craft within his reach.

In beginning the print block work a square or rectangular surface may be cut into a pleasing group of standard shapes involving straight lines and then simple curves. There may follow at later intervals in the course problems of increasing difficulty consistent with the ability to think and execute. Continued observation of commercial prints and, if possible, of fine handicraft is always in order.

In connection with block printing may well come an early lesson in setting colors.

In color printing the color should be a part of the fiber of the goods without the least injury or change in the texture. Any process which gums the fiber or destroys the texture is not beautiful in its results, and does not give true color printing.

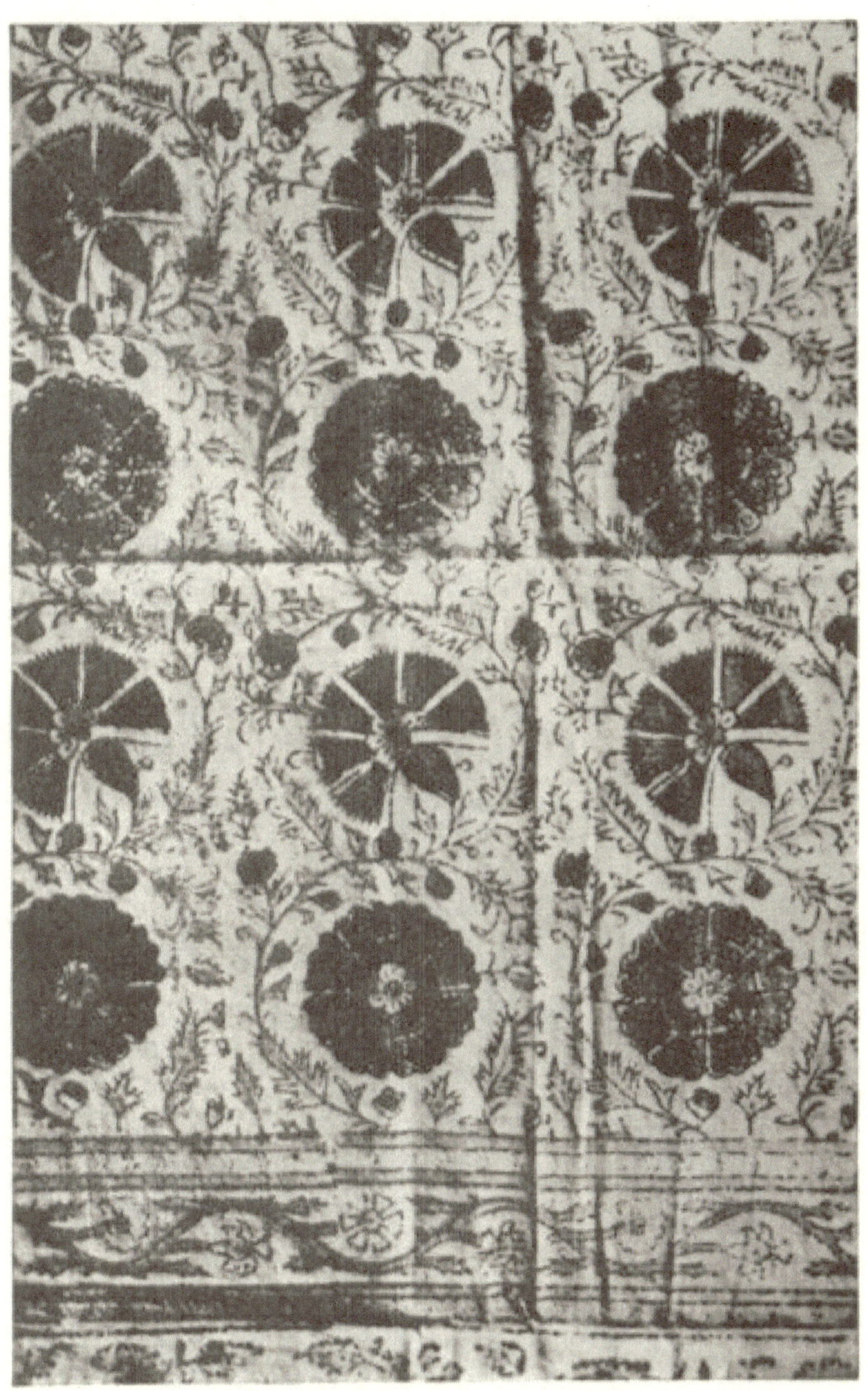

HINDU BLOCK PRINTED DESIGN

PATTERNS FOR PRINT BLOCKS

PRINT BLOCKS, PLAIN AND CUT. PRINT SHOWING INFLUENCE OF STICK PRINTING AND BLOCK PRINTING

Besides the method elsewhere referred to, the following will give excellent results in block printing. A large tin cover into which a thick piece of felt is fitted serves as a color pad. Pains should be taken to have the right quantity of dye well spread on the pad. Too much color makes the printing less clear. When a trial on a piece of the goods is right a large number of imprints can then be made. The secret of good work is a nice adjustment of the color pad and then uniformity of pressure on the block, both in taking color from the pad and in making the imprint. The printing is done on a flat surface with a single layer of blotter beneath the textile. Some fabrics take the imprint better if slightly dampened.

The illustration of block printing is a specimen of Hindu work.

The sticks will find continued use in printing connecting spots and for the introduction of additional color so often needed for enrichment.

The manufactured textile here illustrated was designed by using stick printing and block printing.

When the attainment reached with sticks and print blocks is sufficient to call for larger and more varied design, it is time for the craft to broaden and include stenciling.

Stenciling is the most exacting master of simplicity. It teaches one how to sweep away all that is trivial and unnecessary in design. It shows the value of broad, flat tones combined with accurate drawing, and proves conclusively the vital importance of good composition.

The stenciling process has been described so many times that directions for the work are not needed. An elementary lesson in all-over dyeing can very appropriately be given in connection with advanced block printing or stenciling. This might well be the waxing over of the printed or stenciled pattern, followed by a dipping for the ground color.

The example of stenciling illustrated is a table cover. The material is natural colored linen. The colors were liquid dyes blown on with an atomizer. The bodies, heads and legs of the cranes are orange; the wings and tails blue. The flowers and spots are purple, the leaves and stems blue.

Spraying liquid dye with an atomizer permits not only of the usual direct coloring of the design areas, but also of resist stenciling, in which a light design is produced on a dark background. A small dark design on a large light background is stringy and thin. The light seems to eat into the edge of the design and minimize its importance. On the other hand, a small light design on a large dark background is magnified in importance. While for proper control in either case we must adjust the space relations of the design and background areas, yet it is equally important that one be able to adjust the color relations of the design and background areas.

STENCIL DESIGNS. APPLIED STENCIL PATTERN

The process for "resist" stenciling is as follows: The stencil is laid upon the surface to be decorated, and the open pattern is carefully covered with a thin layer of library paste or paste made from flour and salt water. Flour added to a solution of salt in water is the best preparation we have found. A palette knife, or a case knife may be used to spread this paste. The stencil is at once lifted and the color desired for the background is sprayed in a flat tone over the entire surface. The paste acts as a resist, preventing the penetration of the color. The entire surface is immediately wet with cold water and the resist washed off. The stencil is carefully and thoroughly cleaned in the same way and then pressed and dried.

STENCIL DESIGNS

This is especially suitable for book covers and end paper designs, or mats, where the pattern does not partake of the nature of a repeat, as it is better to remove the resist while wet.

It is interesting to stencil the open pattern in one or more colors, then apply the resist and give another color to the background.

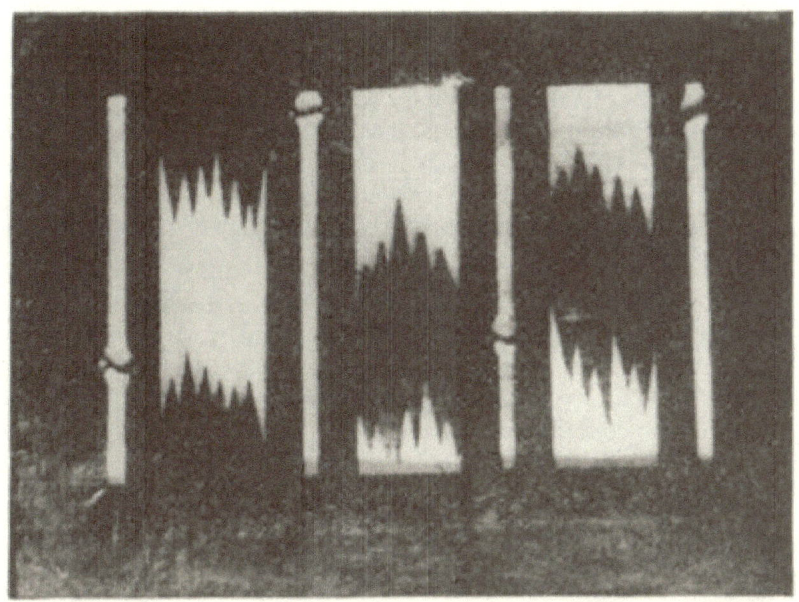

OLD JAPANESE STENCILS

Most interesting stenciling has been done with two or more stencils. To make these, a stencil should be cut for each color. Use the original design sheet for one color. Transfer other color areas to new sheets. Make all sheets, including the tracing paper, the same size. Before tracing lay sheets and tracing paper together and punch coinciding holes in the upper corners. Keep these holes coincident during the process of tracing. By means of these holes the respective stencils are easily applied so that the color scheme is accurately reproduced.

It must not be overlooked by those who are stenciling that only part of the color applied becomes incorporated into the fiber of the goods. The other part is outside the fiber, adherent to the goods. This adherent color should be removed. It corresponds to the excess color in dyeing, which we take pains to remove by rinsing. The very purpose of the steaming, or other "setting" process, is to incorporate the dye into the fiber. This is never perfectly accomplished. There is always some excess adherent color to be removed.

How often we meet the following experience: A craft worker in decorating a fabric applies color until the eye is pleased, takes little or no pains to incorporate the color into the fiber, and ignores altogether the fact that some of the color is only adherent. Later this adherent color comes off (not out) in the wash. There is then disappointment and complaint against methods, colors, etc., when the real fault is one of workmanship. Adherent color is never dependable.

The Japanese have been the masters of the art of stenciling. The technique and beauty of their designs have not been equalled by any other craftsmen. For centuries these people have been making imprints on fabrics.

The old stencils are more simple and the paper of better quality. These old stencils are always darkened by time.

The stencils shown in the illustration were collected by Ernest Fenollosa, an authority on Japanese art.

Little has been written about these stencils but many museums and school art departments have collections.

In cutting stencils the Japanese use a number of tools. Some of these tools are of the nature of punches, being the shape of the cut out place. There is no drawing on the stencil paper, the workman looks at the design and cuts the pattern free hand. The paper, before cutting, is treated with oil and a kind of lacquer.

The old stencils were strengthened by a net work of human hair placed between two stencils cut at the same time. These stencils were then pasted together with rice paste. This net work of hair serves as ties in the stencil and permits a larger freedom of design than is otherwise possible.

The Japanese use two methods for stenciling, the direct coloring method, in which the dye is brushed on the material through the stencil, and the resist method, in which a paste is rubbed through the stencil on the white goods and the fabric dyed in an all-over bath. The color is set by steaming and the paste washed out. This leaves a white pattern on a colored background.

INDEX

A

All-Over Dyeing *V, 21, 25, 50, 68, 86, 92*

B

Basic Colors *27*
Batik Frame *32*
Batiks In Holland *7*
Block Printing *Viii, 25, 26, 40, 86, 87, 88, 91, 92*

C

Costume Jewelry *Viii, 50, 51*
Crackle *3, 8, 45, 53, 57, 60*

D

Direct Colors *26*
Dyeing Over Old Color *30*
Dyes *26, 27, 29, 37*

E

End Papers *V, Viii, 7, 50*

M

Miniature Stages *66*

O

Old Batik Designs *13, 14, 15, 16, 17, 18, 19, 20*

P

Pattern Dyeing *Iii, Iv, V, Vi, 23, 25, 26, 27, 37, 68, 86*
Petroplast Ornaments *54*
Plays And Pageants *65, 68*
Principles Of Dyeing *21*

R

Resist Stenciling *92*

S

Sarongs *50, 64*
Shaded Dyeing *24*
Sizing *22*
Stencil Dyeing *86*
Stick Printing *26, 40, 80, 86, 88, 91, 92*
Stick Tying *80, 81, 82, 83, 85*
Sulphur Colors *27*

T

Tie-Dyed Work *25, 26, 75, 76, 77, 80*
Tjanting *6, 7, 37, 50, 57*
Tjap *6, 7, 50*

V

Vat Dyes *27*
Vegetable Colors *28*

W

Wax Resist Processes *Viii, 31*

Now what I want to do is to put definitely before you a cause for which to strive. That cause is the Democracy of Art, the ennobling of daily and common work, which will one day put hope and pleasure in the place of fear and pain as the forces which move men to labor and keep the world a-going.

·····William Morris

Lector House believes that a society develops through a two-fold approach of continuous learning and adaptation, which is derived from the study of classic literary works spread across the historic timeline of literature records. Therefore, we aim at reviving, repairing and redeveloping all those inaccessible or damaged but historically as well as culturally important literature across subjects so that the future generations may have an opportunity to study and learn from past works to embark upon a journey of creating a better future.

This book is a result of an effort made by Lector House towards making a contribution to the preservation and repair of original ancient works which might hold historical significance to the approach of continuous learning across subjects.

HAPPY READING & LEARNING!

LECTOR HOUSE LLP
E-MAIL: lectorpublishing@gmail.com

www.ingramcontent.com/pod-product-compliance
Lightning Source LLC
LaVergne TN
LVHW090008200726
843493LV00004B/811